Blossom

A 30-Day Journey for the Single Mom

by Elaina Michelle

Blossom
A 30-Day Journey for the Single Mom by Elaina Michelle
Copyright© 2017 Elaina Michelle

Contact the author for bulk orders or requests at
michelleelaina@hotmail.com

Edited by Val Pugh-Love

Cover design by Kanika Harris

Publishing coordination by Brown & Duncan Brand

ISBN 978-0-9984756-6-0

Printed in the United States of America

Dedication

To my daughter, Alyssa, my beauty for ashes.

Acknowledgements

To Alyssa, you are my biggest supporter. Thank you for believing in me when I didn't believe in myself. Your sweet words and warm hugs are forever engrained in my heart. Your patience and your love, during those late nights and long talks, pushed me to never give up. It is an honor to be your mother and watch you blossom I love you more than words can say.

To my mom, Junette, you support and love me in ways I'll never understand. I am forever grateful that even when life was hard you never gave up on being my mom. Your triumph is my platform. Thank you for the countless prayers you prayed over me throughout the years. You are extraordinary.

To Sarah Kang and Andrea Payne dear sisters in Christ, you listened, you prayed, and you supported me more than you know. I am forever grateful for your prayers. Thank you for always being authentic and real.

To Melissa Alvarez, you always keep it real. The journey with you has been epic. You have challenged me to stretch and grow in ways I never thought possible. It has been a blessing to know you and share my heart with you. Thank you for opening your life to me and for loving my family as your own.

To Angie Evenrud, I am so blessed by what God has allowed to grow through our friendship. We have shared joys, pains, and everything in between. We are forever connected through our bond as single mothers. Thank you for your loyalty and support.

To Bettitina Brown, as a child, I watched you grow into a mighty woman of God. It's an honor to know you. No matter when I've called and no matter what question I've asked you've always spoke life to my spirit. Thank you for being available and for being an encouraging presence throughout this process.

To Val, I'm so grateful to have crossed paths with you. This was my baby and you were so graceful and caring with my questions and concerns. Your support in the message of this book has been uplifting. Thank you for being dedicated to making this manuscript its best through your edits.

Blossom

A 30-Day Journey for the Single Mom

Preface

The weight of single motherhood can be a heavy one. It's a weight that only other single mothers can truly understand. We've become very good at putting on smiles and making it look easy. Meanwhile, in the process, we've given up some of the most beautiful parts of who God created us to be. On the contrary, if you look close enough, you'll find that your eyes are still holding onto the visions of things you've long let go of in your heart. What are you hoping for right now? Are you believing God for something that you can't see? Do you know that there is greatness within you waiting to be birthed?

Everything God designed you to be, everything He designed you to do, and every dream He gave you is still alive within you! While single motherhood may not have been a destination you planned for in your journey, it is hardly a wasted one. You have not been counted out of God's family. His love for you is relentless, and He deeply desires to partner with you.

If you are reading this book, it is not by accident. I strongly believe that you are here right now because you know deep down inside that God has more for you. Single mom to single mom, I wrote this book for you. You are not alone, and your life is far from being over. For the next 30 days, you're going to be encouraged, stretched, and tickled straight into the arms of Jesus. My prayer is that, as a single mom, you will be empowered towards your greatness as you intentionally connect with God. Every birth starts with a seed that has been sown and cared for. Today, you have the opportunity to grab a hold of something that you thought was dead and watch it burst forth into something more beautiful than what you thought could exist. Single motherhood did not kill it, and your child did not take it away. That seed is still there waiting to be nurtured. Are you ready to *Blossom*?

Introduction

As a single mom, I'm all too aware that it can feel like time isn't always on your side. No worries! These chapters have been designed with you in mind. Each chapter will begin with a look into my own journey and thoughts as a single mom (the good, the bad, and the ugly) with a Biblical perspective. The rest of the chapter is broken down into bite-sized pieces tailored to make your experience more personal. Here's what you can look forward to:

~**Let's Break It Down** will use what, where, when, why, and how to break down the chapter information in applicable ways so that you can see it in action in your daily life.

~**Let's Connect It to Scripture** will highlight Bible verses pertaining to the chapter and encourage further study of the Bible.

~**Let's Walk It Out** provides a moment for you to stop, pray, and hear from God on a more intimate level. An area for your signature and date is also provided in this section as a form of accountability and commitment to your new journey.

~**Let's Write It Out** offers two to three questions meant to engage you in the chapter, help you foster deeper thought, and create actions or goals based on what you've read.

~**Let's Pray It Out** provides a simple prayer to end your devotional time.

I know you will be amazed at your progress over the next thirty days. Getting to know God, yourself, and who you are in Him is the secret sauce to becoming the woman He created you to be. Don't let anything hold you back from what God has for you. Allow this book to inspire you as you navigate through hills and valleys over the next thirty days. Let hope rise in your heart, and then give it wings so it can fly. I'd love to hear from you! Please contact me at michelleelaina@hotmail.com and let me know how this book has impacted you.

Blessings,
Elaina

Day One

Make God the Most Important Part of Your Day

Sometimes it seems like the days of a single mom never end. It's as if they almost run together and the sun and the moon are just there to give a pretty background to your hectic life. Each day brings endless to-do lists, piles of laundry, helping with homework, wiping tears, telling stories, tickling sessions, and dinner in thirty minutes! (Am I alone in feeling like my autopilot switch is always on?) With days like these, it can be hard to find time for yourself, let alone time for anything else outside of work and motherhood. I'm sure that the day your child(ren) was born, that precious, screaming angel became the most important thing in your world. It's no wonder your days tend to revolve around them. However, a change of perspective on what's most important could greatly enhance your entire life.

Lately, I've taken a keen interest to gardening. Just the mere idea that we have been given the ability through Christ to work the land and bring forth food is fascinating for me! My very first attempt was with a pot of basil. Now, when I brought this herb home, it was brightly colored, big, and thriving. Unfortunately, within a week, it was nearly dead. I had picked and picked at it to go with meals to eat. I enjoyed it for the first few days. Yet, I had not been wise in how I picked at it, and I completely forgot to pay attention to its need for adequate sun and water. Thus, I had stunted its growth. We are much like that pot of basil. As mothers, we smell heavenly and add love and flavor to everything we touch. However, sometimes we're so busy giving of ourselves that we neglect our own care. Before we know it, we've stunted our own growth. Consequently, we're tired, grumpy, and slow.

Did you know that there is a better way to operate in the beautiful madness of your everyday life? It begins by making God the most important part of your day. This may be something new to you, but I assure you that it is life-changing. God is not like any earthly father. He does not require that you perform perfectly in order to receive His love, forgiveness, and salvation. There is nothing you can do or will be able to ever do in the future that will cause Him to make you earn His love. His love is a free gift available to anyone who would truly receive it. I'm telling you this so that you will see why He should be the most important part of your day. In order to keep that pot of basil alive and thriving, I needed to keep it connected to its main sources of life, namely proper water and sun. It is the same with you. In order to be a mom who is thriving, you must stay connected to your main source – Jesus. You should strive to stay connected to God through a personal relationship with Jesus. This is the bread and butter of your life as a believer.

If you haven't already figured (I'm sure you will soon), life is a wild ride that is full of unexpected twists, turns, and drops. At best, it's smart to just strap in and enjoy the ride as much as you can. Who is guiding your ride? Who is your seatbelt? There is only one that knows all, including you and your life. He makes good plans for you. He can also warn you and advise you. However, if you are not connecting with Him daily, how can you know His plans? How can you know when to go or when to be still? When you make God the most important part of your day, you not only get to experience His life giving presence, but you also get the inside scoop on things He desires to share with you. Over time, the moment in your day devoted wholly to God will develop into something grand and gorgeous. You will find that hours feel like mere minutes, and you will no longer watch the clock because you will be face-to-face with God.

Let's Break it Down:

How: Make God the most important part of your day by intentionally setting time aside daily to spend with Him in prayer, in worship, in His Word, and listening to Him.

When: Since you are making God the most important part of your day, I encourage you to choose a time of day that is important to you. Generally, if your day starts in the morning when you get up, this would be the best time because your time with Him will set the tone for the day before anything or anyone else has a chance to do so.

Where: You can be very creative with where you choose to spend time with God. If it's sunny outside, you can head to the park or your porch. Maybe you have a favorite room or chair. It really doesn't matter where you choose, and it doesn't always have to be the same place every time. Just make sure it is a place that is free of personal distraction, and it is comfortable for you. This is your time with God, so make it special.

What: In my church we call our time with God "Facetime." Nevertheless, the bottom line is that this is your daily date with your Provider, your Protector, and your Friend. Grab your Bible, a journal, and a pen. Then, put on some praise music and hang out with God. You can talk about anything you want. You can cry and vent frustrations. You can even ask for help! If this is new to you, don't worry. It's easy to get started. Download the Bible app on your phone. They have many ready to go devotions, or you can start reading the book of John which will help you connect with Jesus as your Savior. Use a music app to find a good praise music playlist if you are unfamiliar with or new to Christian music. Then, commit to at least spending 3-5 minutes each day with Jesus.

Why: God longs to be in relationship with you. He longs to walk through life with you and help you become all that He created you for. Whether you have realized it or not, as His child, you naturally long to be connected to Him as well, and this is the way that it happens.

Let's Connect it to Scripture:

♥ Matthew 6:33 - "But seek first his kingdom and his righteousness, and all these things will be given to you as well."
♥ John 15:5 - "Yes, I am the vine; you are the branches. Those who remain in me, and I in them, will produce much fruit. For apart from me you can do nothing."
♥ Acts 17:28 - "For in him we live and move and exist. As some of your own poets have said, 'We are his offspring.'"
♥ Psalm 16:5 - "Lord you alone are my inheritance, my cup of blessing. You guard all that is mine."
♥ Psalm 32:8 - "The Lord says, 'I will guide you along the best pathway for your life. I will advise you and watch over you.'"

Let's Walk it Out:

Now's the time to intentionally decide when you will set time aside for God in your day. Remember, He is your #1 priority. Your relationship with Him must be put before anything else in order for you to thrive. Use the lines below to write out your plan for daily time with God.

_____

_____

_____

_____

_____

_____

Sign_____

Date_____

Make God the Most Important Part of Your Day

Let's Write it Out:

1. What has today's scriptures revealed to you about who God is?

2. What is one way you feel that spending daily time with God will help you?

3. What is the hardest thing to understand about God as your main lifesource? Pray and ask God to make it plain and simple for you to understand.

Let's Pray it Out:

Lord, my days can get really busy, and sometimes it's easy for me to put you on the backburner of my life. Today, I declare that I will choose to make my relationship with you a priority. Forgive me for neglecting you and not making you the most important part of my day. Lord, it is my desire to stay in continual connection with you. Thank you for allowing me to have all I need in you. Amen.

Day Two

Refresh Yourself

I am always excited for the weekend. After a long and busy week, it's nice to know that there's a break in the hectic pace coming up ahead. Ironically, studies have shown that when you're unable to properly shift from a stress mode to a relaxation mode, you can experience heart disease, diabetes, headaches, depression, digestion, and even accelerated aging. I know this is a terrible list, and surely no one wants to suffer from any one of these. However, before you run for the face cream and probiotics, stop and really think about what you have allowed stress to do to you. Then take a moment to savor the delight of knowing there is another way to manage your stress.

As a daughter of the King this is not how your Daddy intended for you to walk through life. In fact, it's the exact opposite. When you are riddled with ailments from the stresses of life, it can easily distract you from the things God wants to do in you and through you. This is why you always need to have a plan for how you will keep yourself refreshed. Yes, even single mamas deserve time to themselves. I realize you've got mouths to feed, hugs to give, and lessons to teach. On the contrary, if you really think about it, how effective can you be for your children or anyone else if you never stop, if you're always on the go, or if you're always doing for others and never for yourself? God thinks you are amazing, but He knows you're not perfect, and He doesn't even expect you to be. Therefore, it's time that you start treating yourself like the amazing woman He created you to be, instead of the cold, hard-wired robot with no needs or feelings that you've been pretending to be.

I'm always in awe of our bodies and how God so magnificently designed them. If we ever stopped to listen and pay attention to our bodies, we'd be amazed at the findings. Did you know that when you feel fatigued, it's actually a sign built into your body to alert you that you need rest? Another interesting fact is that inflammation in the body is actually a protective mechanism to alert the body that something is not right. Have you had any of those feelings lately? If you're going to be a rock star mom raising world-changers, then you've got to start taking care of yourself.

God created the Heavens and the Earth in seven days, and then He rested. My point here is that if God, our Mighty Creator who doesn't even need to rest, can stop and take one, then surely you even as a single mom can humble yourself and rest, too. You were not designed to operate at a non-stop, back-breaking pace. When you do operate in that manner, it's really just blocking God's power from working in and through you. You're operating in an I-can-do-it-all attitude, when the truth is you can't do it all. No one can. So, feel free to take a much needed breather. Refresh yourself in the Lord, and be renewed.

Let's Break it Down:

How: This does not require a perfect plan; it's really all about you. Relax however you want. Stop and listen to your body. Turn off the robot and get in tune with how you really feel physically and emotionally. Do something you really enjoy or something you've never done before. Are your muscles achy and tense? Maybe a massage or a hot bath will be what you need. Have you been inactive physically? Consider taking a brisk walk or playing tag with the kids to get your blood pumping. Have you been feeling bored with your routine? Shake things up with a new activity such as a Pinterest craft. Have you lost touch with your girlie side? Paint your nails, get a pedicure, or give your hair or face some love with a sweet smelling mask. Do you need a mini-getaway? Grab a book and a quiet place or find a nearby monument to visit. This is another place where you can feel free to get creative.

What: This is when you really need to focus in on your body. How are you feeling? Complete an assessment of all your senses. Are you mentally drained? Physically exhausted? Spiritually hungry? Pray about it and ask God to reveal to you where you most need refreshing right now. This means that refreshment could look different for you depending on what's going on in your life. Release the need to be everything, and allow yourself to be vulnerable before the Lord so that He can speak to you.

When: Get refreshed whenever you feel like you need it. There's no right or wrong time. If you know that you'll explode if you don't get some time to yourself at least once a week, that's great. Schedule that time into your week and make it happen. If by mid-week you're crashing, squeeze a mini-refresher into the middle of your week. It can be something small that gives you that extra charge - kind of like a catnap. It gets you going again and leaves you looking forward to that big unwind at the end of the week. Make refreshing specific to you, your lifestyle, and your schedule. Then, make sure it happens.

Where: Refresh wherever you want. Use your creative imagination. I mean, if you literally just get three minutes in the bathroom by yourself, go ahead and say a quick prayer asking for refreshment. Then, walk out of that bathroom like royalty ready to go. Refreshment could happen at the park. It's nearly impossible to not feel refreshed when you are surrounded by God's beautiful creation. Don't be closed off to the many random possibilities that the Lord may provide to you for refreshment.

Why: There are so many reasons why taking time to get refreshed is important. Feel free to make your reasons personal. Get refreshed for your children, for your future husband, for the neighbor, or for the coworker that God wants you to encourage. Most importantly, do it for yourself. Do it because God always has your best interest in mind, and He is more than capable of handling the details of your life. Take your rest in His arms and feel refreshed.

Let's Connect it to Scripture:

♥ Isaiah 40:31 – "But those who trust in the Lord will find new strength. They will be strong like eagles soaring upward on wings; they will walk and run without getting tired."
♥ Psalms 4:8 – "In peace I will lie down and sleep, for You alone, O Lord, will keep me safe."
♥ Matthew 11:28 – "Then Jesus said, 'Come to me, all of you who are weary and carry heavy burdens, and I will give you rest.' "
♥ Psalm 23:1-13 – "The Lord is my Shepherd; I have all that I need. He lets me rest in green meadows; He leads me beside peaceful streams. He renews my strength. He guides me along right paths bringing honor to His name."
♥ John 10:10 – "The thief's purpose is to steal and kill and destroy. My purpose is to give them a rich and satisfying life."
♥ Ephesians 2:10 – "For we are God's masterpiece. He has created us anew in Christ Jesus, so we can do the good things He planned for us long ago."

Let's Walk it Out:

Here's the time to be intentional. If you haven't already, take the time now to pray and ask for God's leading in your refreshment. Use the lines below to write out when you'll stop to rest and refresh this week and how.

_____

_____

_____

_____

_____

_____

Sign_____

Date_____

Refresh Yourself

Let's Write it Out:

1. What has today's scriptures revealed to you about who God is?

2. What do you think may be some roadblocks that would keep you from getting your personal refreshment? How do you plan to overcome these roadblocks? Pray about this.

3. What are the top two reasons that you would benefit from taking time to regularly get refreshed?

Let's Pray it Out:

Lord Jesus, you are magnificent and wonderful in all your ways. I pray that you would help me to stop and take time to allow myself to be refreshed. Even when it seems like I have too much to do to stop and rest, I pray that you would remind me that You are in control and that I can trust You to help me with everything. Forgive me for my I-can-do-it-all attitude. Thank you that I can always come to you for rest. Amen.

Day Three

Get A Mentor

As a child, I was very quiet and reserved. I laughed little and showed very little emotions. I always felt like I was in the background of life just hanging out watching everyone else have a ball. I never looked at myself and thought that there was anything special or unique enough about me to stand out. Beyond the glasses and braces, I always felt like a shadow. Then, my fifth grade teacher noticed me. I will never forget her name or that moment in time. I can still see the classroom-trailer I was sitting in when I was in her class. I remember her hair and the soft, kind way she looked at me. She saw me, and she spoke life into me. From that moment, a season began where she would continually affirm the gift she saw in me, and she would encourage me in it. I was able to open up to her and share a piece of me that I was still trying to understand and get to know. She helped awaken that gift in me by calling it out, and a foundation was laid that later would birth something I would share over and over again in my life. I did not know it at the time, but this was my very first encounter with a mentor.

Later in life, I would shy away from the idea of a mentor because I thought having a mentor meant that I didn't have my stuff together. The pride in me at that time did not want to appear weak. Little did I know, this mindset was purely a lie from the enemy to keep me stuck in my mess and not growing. Now, I want to take some time to differentiate a few things here. First, no one has it together so well that they don't need a mentor. So, let's break off pride or shame right now in the name of Jesus. Secondly, the type of mentor I'm focused on is not the one that's going to help you get promoted at your job or teach you how to break open into a new career. While these types of mentors are great, what I'm focused on for you is a spiritual mentor. That leads to me to clearing any confusion there may be between a discipleship relationship and a mentorship relationship.

21

Both of these relationships are a part of a growing Christian woman's life, and you must know which relationship is for you in your current season of life. Not only that, but you must also determine if you are ready to be mentored. Let's discover the differences. We'll cover mentoring first. One of my favorite Biblical examples of a mentoring relationship is between Naomi and her daughter-in-law Ruth. I love Ruth's story. If you haven't already done so, I encourage you to read the book of Ruth. Naomi was an older, wiser woman of God who had many life experiences to draw from to provide advice and counsel to her daughter-in-law. Ruth was a younger woman with little experience in comparison to Naomi. Naomi and Ruth formed a relational experience, and through that, Naomi was able to empower Ruth to be the woman that God had called her to be. Naomi shared her God-given knowledge and resources with Ruth. She was able to closely supervise her and provide her with correction, encouragement, and individualized help specific to her life and season. Now, Ruth could've been a hardheaded, mean, and stubborn know-it-all. Read her story, and you'll find that it was quite the opposite. She was a caring, hard-working, and humble servant. It's a good thing, too, because had Ruth not been easy to mentor, she would never have reached her God-sized destiny.

In a mentoring relationship, both the mentor and the mentee must be willing to open up their lives to each other and to be committed, transparent, and grounded in the Word. To be a mentee, you must be teachable. This is not a relationship where you just sit back and listen to someone give you lectures. You must be able to be receptive to hearing difficult things. You also must be someone who is honest and trustworthy to keep conversations confidential and to tell the truth about yourself even if it's not pretty. Most importantly, you must be ready to take action, to study, and to reflect. A mentoring relationship can become a drain if the mentee is not willing to actually do the work that is required. For that reason, while being mentored, try to show your mentor that you are thankful and appreciate the time they are taking to invest into your growth and development. Ask how you can pray for them, send flowers, or pay for lunch sometimes. These little things may seem silly, but they will really bless your mentor.

Discipleship is also a relational experience. However, the difference is that in a discipleship relationship, the disciple is always a more mature Christian who takes the time to walk alongside a newer Christian to help them understand their new commitment to the Lord and how to walk with Jesus. Most churches have developed their own discipleship program, and it will usually start at the very basics of who Jesus is and what He did for us. It will continue through a series of foundational Christian principles. Every new Christian should start with a discipleship relationship, and then at its successful conclusion, a mentorship can be formed. This can be with the same person or a different one if you desire. The important thing is not to shy away from either one. Both relationships play a pivotal role in your growth and development.

Let's Break it Down:

How: Forming a mentoring relationship is easy. I would suggest you first start by praying and asking God to highlight a woman in your church that would be a good fit. Keep in mind that you may end up asking a couple of women before you finally find a mentor. Don't be discouraged by this or fear rejection. Just believe that their "no" means God has a better-fitted person in mind or that God needs you to get your attitude in check first. I personally asked several women over the course of a few months until I found someone to mentor me. What's funny is that it was a woman that I had determined I didn't want to really be close with at the time. It's funny how God works. When I shared that with her over one of our meet-ups, she first wanted to know what it was about her that made me feel that way. This was for her own reflection and growth. Then, she smiled and commented that usually when feelings like that arise in this type of relational situation, it's the enemy trying to keep that relationship from forming. The enemy knows that the relationship has God written all over it, and that it is destined to bring forth major fruit.

What: Please make sure that it is the time in your life to be mentored and not the time for a discipleship. Once you have your mentor, they'll most likely want to know what's going on in your life and why you want to be mentored. Don't be bashful about it. Just be honest.

When: Determining a schedule of when to meet should be based off both of your schedules. There is no rule set in stone for when mentors should meet with their mentees. It can be weekly, bi-weekly, or even quarterly depending on your need and the availability of both you and your mentor. Also, the meetings don't always have to be in person. I prefer face-to-face contact, but some situations may call for just a phone call, a Skype, or even a text. Between the two of you, determine the boundaries for your relationship.

Where: The biggest rule here is to pick a place where both of you will be comfortable. It could be at a coffee shop, a bookstore, the park, or alternating between each other's homes. In my opinion, the location doesn't require complete silence. However, it should at least be a place where you can talk without having to raise your voice, and you should be able to give each other your complete focus and attention.

Why: If you desire a mentor, then I'm sure you've figured out the reason. Understand that your mentor is not going to do any work for you. She is simply going to seek God on your behalf and draw out of you what she sees in you so that you can grow and go to the next level in your life. Please only seek out female mentors for spiritual growth. This one is serious. The first reason is because a male will not have the same life experience to help you since he has been walking around this earth as a man. Secondly, picking a male as a mentor can open the door for the enemy to mess with both of your minds. It's highly likely that the relationship will become perverted in some way, and you'll end up worse off than when you started. Please, please heed this advice and only work with female mentors.

Let's Connect it to Scripture:

♥ Ecclesiastes 4:10 – "If one person falls, the other can reach out and help. But someone who falls alone is in real trouble."
♥ Hebrews13:7 – "Remember your leaders who taught you the Word of God. Think of all the good that has come from their lives, and follow the example of their faith."
♥ Proverbs13:20 – "Walk with wise and become wise; associate with fools and get in trouble."
♥ Psalm145:4 – "Let each generation tell its children of your mighty acts; let them proclaim your power."

Let's Walk it Out:

Now that you understand what mentoring is and why we all need a mentor, are you ready to take the next step? Take some time to pray and ask God to reveal to you if you're in a season where you need to be mentored or if you need to be a part of a discipleship. Ask God to highlight a woman that is a mature Christian who could walk with you. Use the lines below to write what God says to you.

_____

_____

_____

_____

_____

_____

Sign _____

Date_____

Let's Write it Out:

1. What have today's scriptures revealed to you about who God is?

2. What are some possible issues of your heart that God may want you to deal with before beginning a mentorship? Pray about this and ask God for His help.

Let's Pray it Out:

Father, you are excellent in all of your ways. Thank you for providing an example of how we should all strive to grow in our faith. I pray that you would prepare my heart so that I can thrive in my mentorship relationship just as Ruth did. It is my desire to be the woman that you designed me to be. I ask that you would help me to get rid of any pride or shame, and I pray that your promises would always be in my heart. Amen.

Day Four

Find Something You Enjoy Doing

As a single mom, it can seem like your life becomes all about your children. Even in a 24-hour day, somehow everything you think and do becomes connected to your children. It's true that you often have to perform double duties as a single mom. It can be daunting to fill a role that was designed for two. However, because you're a fighter, resilient, and you love your kids, you've developed a way to manage the stress of running a single-parent household. Now, there is nothing wrong with that. In fact, it's admirable and it's what makes single moms so courageous and so strong. So, I'm sure you're wondering why are we discussing why you need to find something you enjoy doing? I'm glad you asked, because I can tell you in one word...balance.

We're good at balancing our schedule, balancing tasks, and balancing our emotions. Though, the one thing single moms usually let slip through the cracks is keeping ourselves balanced. This small change could truly enhance your quality of life and even help reduce your stress. Too many single moms find themselves so completely lost in their child(ren) that when they stop to take a breather, they realize that they have no idea who they are. Don't feel bad if this has happened to you. We all have the best intentions when it comes to our kids, and sometimes we all need a little reminder that we are actually a living, breathing woman who has desires, dreams, and thoughts. Just because you have kids now does not mean your life is over. Your child(ren) are essentially an extension of your team. While you may not be married, you're still co-coaching (co-parenting) with God. Understand that a coach is a person, not a programmed robot. A coach guides, leads, nurtures, and provides discipline and accountability. A coach does not eat, sleep, breath their players 24/7. In fact, a coach needs downtime to recharge, re-strategize, and still enjoy a life of being who they are.

This is why it's important to find something that you enjoy doing. You are a single mom, but that is not the beginning and end of who you are.

You are that and then some! It's time for you to reconnect with yourself. It's time for you to find balance in your hectic life. In order for you to be the best mother that you can be, you first need to know who you are as a mother and as a woman. First, remember that your identity is found only in Jesus. Accordingly, if you're not sure who you are, then the first place to go is to Him. He already knows all your talents, skills, and fears. He's completely aware of all your needs and desires. Please do not seek to find your identity through social media or your favorite TV show. You were not designed as a copycat of someone else. Everything you have has been given to you for a purpose, and this is why it's important for you to be able to connect with who you are. God can use you outside of your home and kids. Still, in order for Him to do that, you must be aware of who you are, what you're good at, and where you need improvement.

In all, finding something that you enjoy doing is a stepping stone to discovering who you are and what you enjoy doing outside of being a mom. For some of you, this may feel so foreign and awkward because maybe you haven't come in contact with the real you for quite some time. That's ok. Don't let that uncomfortableness of this experience scare you away from finding yourself. There's a saying that "great things never came from comfort zones." I totally agree with this, and I encourage you to know that if you're feeling a little uncomfortable, then it means you're growing. Embrace growth and watch as you begin to thrive.

Let's Break it Down:

How: Finding something you enjoy doing is a way to explore how to find balance and how to reconnect with yourself. If you have a favorite hobby or pastime, it may be time to revisit it now. Otherwise, be creative in finding something that sparks your interest. There's so much information out there and resources are easier to reach than ever before. I personally love Pinterest because I can find anything from ideas on outfits to dinner recipes and gardening ideas. Another good place to look is at your local recreation center or YMCA or YWCA. They usually offer classes and other interesting things. Plus, most centers offer childcare at a reasonable price if you need it. There's also a great website, www.meetup.com, that helps you locate groups of people who enjoy doing a particular activity together. There are usually plenty of mommy groups that do fun things together while offering a place to let the kids run wild. These groups are typically free. If you don't see one that interests you, consider starting one of your own. The possibilities are literally endless, and it's a bonus if you're able to connect with some really cool women, too.

What: This is only limited to your imagination. Are you adventurous? Do you love nature? Do you have a special ability to paint what you see? Have you ever wanted to design a t-shirt or make a coffee mug? You choose the what. It doesn't have to be the same every time. Feel free to jump around trying new things. When you stumble upon your sweet spot, you will know. Until then, have fun learning new things or rediscovering something you used to love to do.

Where: This is connected to your what. You may find yourself in a coffee shop penning your thoughts into beautiful poetry. You may even be outside in your backyard or in a community garden nurturing a baby tomato plant. Whatever you enjoy doing, know that where it is doesn't really matter. Just embrace the fact that you are actually reconnecting with yourself and discovering your talents and skills so that God can use you to bless others.

When: Don't delay this idea of seeking Jesus and connecting with yourself. Start now. Start small, but don't put it off. Pick a time and day that suits you best and allows you to fully immerse yourself in the activity. If you must bring the kiddos along, try to find something that at least includes credible and affordable childcare. Remember, this is about balance; therefore, this activity does not have to be once a week. It can be once a month. You can also find a small scale activity that can be done from home and incorporate that into your schedule more often. Then, you can leave the larger outside of the home activities for once or twice a month.

Why: It's important to understand that everything you do or don't do is an overflow into your children. If you are overbearing, not hands-on, very emotional, or show little emotion, it all affects them. Subsequently, finding something you enjoy is as much about you as it about your children. If you're struggling, your children will also struggle either internally or externally. A balanced mother that knows who she is and what she likes is a mom who can teach her kids how to be who God says they are. Doing this is a win-win for you and your family. You get closer to God and position yourself to be used by Him. As a result, your children get to have a rock star mom, and they learn to be who they are in Jesus just by watching you.

Let's Connect it to Scripture:

♥ 2 Thessalonians 1:11 – "So we keep praying for you, asking our God to enable you to live a life worthy of His call. May He give you the power to accomplish all the good things your faith prompts you to do."
♥ Ephesians – "For we are God's masterpiece. He has created anew in Christ Jesus, so we can do the good things He planned for us long ago."
♥ Colossians: 7 – "Let your roots grow down into Him, and let your lives be built on Him. Then, your faith will grow strong in the truth you were taught, and you will overflow with thankfulness."
♥ 1 Corinthians 15:58 – "So dear brothers and sisters, be strong and immovable. Always work enthusiastically for the Lord, for you know that nothing you do for the Lord is ever useless."

Let's Walk it Out:

Learning to keep our lives balanced can be a process. The most important thing is to know who you are. Stop, pray, and ask God to tell you who are. Share His response below:

_____

_____

_____

_____

_____

_____

Sign _____

Date _____

Find Something You Enjoy Doing

Let's Write it Out:

1. What have today's scriptures revealed to you about who God is?

2. What are some labels/lies about yourself that you have believed? List those lies, and then write your identity in Jesus next to them to replace the lies that you have believed.

3. What is at least one way that you can work on adding balance to your life by connecting with yourself outside of being a mom?

Let's Pray It Out:

Lord, I declare that I am a balanced mom. In you, I know who I am, and I am comfortable in my own skin. I will no longer hide behind my children. I pray that you would speak identity over me and that I would flourish under your Fatherly care. Reveal to me how I can create balance in my life as I rediscover myself and what I like. Lord, I ask that you would replace all the lies spoken over me with a fresh showering of your love and promises for me. Amen.

Day Five

Never Stop Growing

My daughter is a huge fan of the popular show *The Biggest Loser*. She will literally find a comfy spot in the house and binge watch it for hours if I let her. Personally, I am not as big of a fan, but on occasion, I will watch an episode or two with her. If you've never watched it, let me just tell you that it is about way more than just losing unsurmountable amounts of weight. When the contestants reach the "ranch," it's because they've reached their last hope. They're battling obesity and losing. *The Biggest Loser* is the last line of defense between them and heart disease, stroke, diabetes, and even death. During interviews, the contestants are always asked how they ended up putting on so much weight. At some point, they always end up admitting that they just gave up and became comfortable with what they had allowed themselves to become.

Let's define *complacency* as that feeling you get of being satisfied with how things are and not really wanting to try and make them better. Complacency has a habit of masking itself as self-satisfaction and it's accompanied by the unawareness of any actual dangers or deficiencies. For the contestants of *The Biggest Loser,* complacency really got the best of them. Their journey on the show is not an easy one. They must endure strenuous workouts, eye-opening doctor visits, and strict diet changes, all while battling the disabling mindsets that have brought them to that very place. In this case, an ounce of prevention really is worth a pound of cure.

Although, I've been discussing weight loss, it is complacency that I want to share with you today. Complacency is a killer, and it can attack every realm of your life if you are not watchful to guard against it. Never get too comfortable with any area of your life that you just stop caring about what happens. It is imperative that you look at your life with the same eyes as God. Yes, He loves you and has a hope and future planned for you. Still, how will you ever walk into His plans for you if you get comfortable in your walk with Him? Likewise, how will you reach your career or academic goals if you never challenge yourself to learn more or lead more? In order to prevent death in any area of your life, you must decide that you will never stop growing.

It is never too late to start growing. You have never gone too far that you are incapable of growth. Like the contestants of *The Biggest Loser*, it may take some time to see the fruits of your growth, especially if you've been living in complacency for a while. Yet, that is not a bad thing. I know that just like the contestants, after you put in some work and see the fruits of your labor, you will feel amazing. Remember, that this life is not your own. You were bought with a price, and everything you have is the Lord's. Don't take that the wrong way. Know that you and your life could not be in better hands. What it does mean is that hopefully out of love and admiration for all that's been done for you, you will desire to reach and use the full potential of what's been entrusted to you. That means that you should be embracing the desire to grow and the courage to push complacency out of the way.

Let's Break it Down:

How: Complacency can easily settle in on the best of us. It's not going to wave at you and announce its presence into your life. Complacency will be subtle and quiet; it may even mask itself as something entirely different. It is your job to be on guard for it, to look for complacency in every area of your life, and to catch it before it has time to settle in your life. Seek the Lord in prayer and ask Him to reveal areas that need some TLC.

What: Complacency is tricky. It has the ability to make you feel completely self-satisfied while being completely unaware of actual danger. This is a big deal. Complacency can actually make you feel so comfortable, warm, and fuzzy within yourself that that you become blind to the fact that your health is in danger, that your career is in jeopardy, or that you're ignoring your kids. The keyword is *self*. The trick of complacency is that it causes you to focus on yourself. Human nature and sin causes us to naturally be selfish people.

When you begin focusing on yourself, you develop tunnel vision. You don't see your kids, and you don't even see God. Moreover, tunnel vision causes you to become comfortable. When you're only focused on yourself, you forget what you're here for. You simply want to coast through life, because you're suddenly not concerned with others. You're only concerned with your own life and making yourself feel good and being comfortable. This feeling is to the detriment of everyone else around you, and it causes every other relationship around you to starve.

Where: As I stated before, complacency can invade any area of your life - your career, your relationship with your kids, your spiritual growth. Nothing is off limits when it comes to complacency. If this has been an area of struggle for you, then you may have a couple of areas that need immediate attention. Do an inventory of areas you know that you've been lazy in, and match it up to the areas that are revealed to you in prayer.

When: Start dealing with complacency immediately. This is not something to put off for a better time. When it comes to getting important things done, there is never a better time. You must make it happen with whatever time you have.

Why: Make it a point to never stop growing, because it's what God desires for you. Therefore, if you're only spending time with God three times a week, it's time to grow, attack complacency, and determine to seek God daily. Are you still holding onto hurt or grudges from a past relationship or an ugly encounter with a relative? Now is the time to grow. Declare your forgiveness. Take your broken heart to God, give Him all the pain and tears you're holding inside, and allow Him to heal you.

Have you been cooking food that is not so healthy for your family? You can grow in this area, too. Take a healthy cooking class, buy a book on healthy cooking, and feed your family food that is good for their bodies. Do you feel that you're overdue for a promotion or tired of being stuck in the same job position? Let's get growing then. Seek a mentor to help challenge you to the next level or take a course to learn advanced skills. Check yourself quarterly, and make changes whenever needed. You and the things around you will begin to flourish as you become determined to never stop growing.

Let's Connect it to Scripture:

♥ 2 Corinthians 3:18 – "So all of us who have had that veil removed can see and reflect the glory of the Lord - who is the Spirit - makes us more and more like Him as we are changed into His glorious image."
♥ Revelation 3:15-16 – "I know all the things you do, that you are neither hot

nor cold. I wish that were one or the other! But since you are like the luke-warm water, neither hot nor cold, I will spit you out of my mouth!"

♥ Galatians 6:9 – "So let's not get tired of doing what is good. At just the right time we will reap a harvest of blessing if we don't give up."

Let's Walk it Out:

I don't have much of a green thumb, but I do love planting things. There's something exciting about having a hand in creating life. I hope that you are experiencing that same excitement as you think about ways to conquer complacency. Pray and ask God to reveal an area in your life that needs immediate attention. How do you plan to create growth in that area? Write your answers and His response on the lines below.

_____

_____

_____

_____

_____

_____

Sign _____

Date _____

Let's Write it Out:

1. What have today's scriptures revealed to you about who God is?

2. What are some ways that you have been tricked by complacency?

Let's Pray it Out:

Lord, forgive me for getting too complacent in my life. I know that you have big plans for my life, and I will never reach them if I'm not willing to grow. Change my heart and give me a desire to become the woman you designed me to be. I pray that I would continually seek your face to keep things in my life alive and thriving. Thank you for predestining me for greatness. Amen.

Day Six

Get A Vision

Several years ago, I took a life-mapping class through a local church. Until that point, I had never heard of life-mapping. However, I was in a season of self-discovery, and I just had to find out how this class was going to get me steps closer to my purpose. The class took place over a course of three or four days, and the instructor was bubbly and bold with big dreams. We were given a journal loaded with scriptures and multiple tables that would help us to become organizers and strategists in living out our life according to God's perfect plan and will. In one particular session, we started with worship music and were led into prayer in which we asked God to reveal His plan for us. This covered all facets of our life. We prayed and asked God for vision, and then we waited. Afterwards, we journaled everything. Then, we proceeded to clip from magazines anything that we felt we were led to clip (even if it didn't make any sense at the time) and post it to a board. In the end, I walked away with a vision board.

It was a new and delightful experience that has proven to be unforgettable, and I made some new friends in the process. Today, that board is still posted to my wall. Over the years, I've added notes and things to it, but the overall theme hasn't changed much. That was in 2013. Since then, I have grown tremendously, and I am now beginning to see my vision board take life. There are times in my life when I wonder if I can really hear from God. In these moments, looking at my vision board, I am assured that I really, really do hear from Him. In fact, we all do. The trick is that we have to ask, and then we have to be quiet and listen. Not only that, but we have to be ready to take action on whatever God says.

Have you wondered what God's vision for your family is? For your career? For you? That's wonderful because as a child of the living God, I know that you have a desire in your heart to walk out this life the way God intended for you. So, it's time to get a vision! This vision is a lot of things. Essentially, it will encompass who you are and where you're going. Remember, you're dealing with the Almighty and he is not under any obligation to tell you everything. However be assured that if you ask, He will give you an answer. He is your loving Father, after all. His answer may also cast light on those around you, such as your children or other family members, and maybe even people you haven't even met yet.

There are no boundaries with God, so be ready for it to not make total sense to you. That's where faith comes into play. Whatever the vision is, it will reflect God's dream for you. It may be His dream for you for just a season, and it may be partial. It may be big and broad or small and specific. Nevertheless, it will put you on the right path to God's great idea for you since you were growing in your mother's womb.

Let's Break it Down:

How: Remember that your vision is always connected to God. There is no other way. So begin by seeking God, and then stop, wait, and listen. There is no one particular way that God speaks. You may get a word or a picture. You may get a movie, a song, or a Bible verse. It may not make total sense, but it will reveal enough to give you a direction. Be sure to write everything down and date it. There will be times when doubt will creep in, and you will need to look back at this and be encouraged. Next, you can pull out all of your supplies. This includes your markers, stickers, magazines, photos, glue, tape, and whatever else you want to use to put together your vision board.

Don't get picky when choosing your magazines. National Geographic was one of the magazines laid out for selection during my life-mapping class. I thought it was odd, but I looked through it anyways. I ended up cutting out a big eagle and putting it in the center of my board. I had no idea what it meant until about a year ago, which leads me to the next step. Try to refrain from just cutting out things you like or things that look cute. Really look with your spiritual eyes and ask the Holy Spirit to guide you. Allow yourself to be led during this process. Often times, it will be a feeling deep inside that resonates within you. You may not be able to explain it or understand it, but it will pull at you spiritually. Cut those things out.

What: Getting a vision keeps you from going through life haphazardly. If you have no plan, your life will essentially go nowhere. Furthermore, you will fall victim to the random moving and shaking that happens around you. A vision connects you to the thoughts God has for you. It may expose a new career path or a move into ministry. It may reveal an expansion in your family or some form of blessing He wants to give you. It may define your up-coming spiritual growth or some healing that will take place. When it's time to glue things down into place on your vision board, let the Holy Spirit guide that as well.

In some instances, it may make no difference how it looks when it's all said and done. However, in other cases, it may be necessary to put things in a specific order. Remember, that this is God's plan, not yours. So, don't be thrown off if your vision of whatever God spoke to you doesn't exactly match what you end up cutting out. If you are a control freak or very organized, this would be the time to take authority over those spirits. Otherwise, they may make it difficult for you to really hear.

Where: Putting together your vision board can take place anywhere. Just make sure you have plenty of room to spread out. When it's time to put it up, take some time to think about it. Even pray about it. You want to put it in a place where it will constantly be in your view. Now, I'm not talking about the living room or kitchen, even though I'm sure you spend plenty of time in both places. I'm talking about a space that is personal to you. If you have a prayer closet that you spend daily time in, that would be a great place. You can even put it on your bedroom wall, which is where I have mine. It is important that wherever you put your vision board, is a place where you get to see it every day, maybe even several times a day. This will be your constant and subconscious reminder of what God has in mind for you. When you pray, take time to pray about what is on that board. Ask God for more revelation if something doesn't make sense or more discernment as you make certain choices, so that you may stay in line with His plan.

When: I believe that this can be your choice. Most people stick with a yearly board. Regardless of whatever schedule you decide, it's important to track your progress. Keep a vision board journal to track the progress of things that you complete or things that happen. Consequently, when it's time to make a new one, you will know what needs to be transferred over and what doesn't. Every time you begin another vision board, always make sure you are seeking God for His desired plan and not yours. Take your time putting it together. Don't rush or make other plans that may interfere with its completion. Your goal should be to have the whole thing done and posted up before you stop. When you start it, make a commitment to not get up until it's all done.

Why: I know that after becoming a single mom you may have decided to tuck away your dreams, but God has not given up on you. Therefore, you shouldn't be giving up on yourself or giving up on God. Everything you need to accomplish what He sets before you, is already inside of you. He will provide the open doors, the resources, the money, the people, and anything else you'll need. All you have to do is be bold and step through the door. Trust that even though you don't have a clue how it's all going to happen, it is indeed going to happen. Not only will it happen, but it will be amazing. Once you become comfortable with it, get the kids involved if they're old enough. Even if they can't use scissors yet, maybe they can draw. God has a vision that He wants to share with them, too.

Let's Connect it to Scripture:

♥ Proverbs 29:18 – "When people do not accept divine guidance, they run wild. But whoever obeys the law is joyful."
♥ James 2:26 – "Just as the body is dead without breath, so also faith is dead without good works."
♥ John 15:5 – "Yes, I am the vine; you are the branches. Those who remain in me, and I in them, will produce much fruit. For apart from me you can do nothing."
♥ Psalm 12:6 – "The Lord's promises are pure, like silver refined in a furnace, purified seven times over."

Let's Walk it Out:

Now that you're on fire to connect with God for your vision, take some time to get all your supplies ready. Then, decide on a day that you know you will have time to get your vision board done, and write it below. Also, include how frequently you will seek God to get a fresh vision.

_____

_____

_____

_____

_____

_____

Sign _____

Date_____

Let's Write it Out:

1. What have today's scriptures revealed to you about who God is?

2. Has God given you a vision (maybe from your younger years) that you totally forgot about or gave up on?

Let's Pray it Out.

Dear Lord, I am so excited to connect with you and learn your thoughts for my life. Thank you that your promises are always good and true. I pray that my heart would be in sync with yours and that you would give me ears to hear and a heart to obey. Amen.

Day Seven

Make Time for What's Important

Life can get so busy these days. Everyone and everything seems to move faster and faster as the time goes by. I long for slower, quieter days that are spent outside on the porch surrounded by the giggles and the laughter of little children. It sounds nice, right? However, instead of experiencing the more tranquil days found in my own imagination, I'm sure what most of us are experiencing is a lot of noise. The endless roam of busy streets, the pounding of sleepless cities, and the exhaustion of trying to get it all done before the sun goes down can be very distracting. As a single mom, you may occasionally get swept up in what other people are doing in their lives in comparison to your own. You probably ask yourself: *How does she keep up that pace and look so great? How does she have time for all the activities and never seem stressed?*

Let me warn you that playing the comparison game is a big NO. Comparison is a complete joy killer. I've been repeating it so much, but it bears reminding that you were put on this earth for a purpose that is for you alone. This means that it is completely pointless to waste time comparing yourself, your life, and your journey to someone else's. No matter what, the enemy will always use comparison to make you feel like you got the short end of the stick. It's much like that saying, "the grass is always greener on the other side." The problem is you're looking at someone's Chapter 20 when you're only on Chapter 4. You have no idea how long it took for their grass to get that green and healthy. You can't even begin to imagine the fertilizer, the water, and the mowing it took to produce the life they have. Not to even mention how many times their grass experienced some sort of death or weeds and had to be repaired to get it back growing.

When a strenuous pace and comparison are hanging out together, they will always cause you to miss out on the spectacular moments happening in your own life. So, be on guard against comparison and learn to make time for what's important. When you begin to focus on what God is doing

45

in your own life, you won't have time to be worried about how someone else is winning in their life. In fact, you will be too overjoyed to even notice. So, as you go through your day, be on the lookout for these important moments. Claim joy and live in expectation of God showing up and showing out in your own life. Even better, ask God to give you visual signs of His affection for you.

If your kids are younger, this is the time to cherish everything that you can. Take pictures and videos. Scrapbook or smashbook anything to keepsake times that will be gone before you know it. In essence, simply slow down and enjoy your life without comparing yourself to others. It's all too easy to notice someone's success and begin to judge or compare your life when you don't have all the facts. Take the narrow road, stay in your lane, and encourage - don't compare.

If you're like me, you consider family to be a priority. Especially as a single mom, family is super important. What you consider family is all up to you. It does not have to only include blood-related individuals. Perhaps there's a family from church that has taken a liking to you and your family, and they've decided to take you under their wing. This is considered family. Whether you've got a ton of family surrounding you, or it's just you and your kids, rest assured that family is important. Keep in mind that the people you consider family should be people you can trust to be there when times are good and when times are really bad. That's why no matter how many different ways you are pulled, it is important to always make time for family.

Life on earth is so short, be careful that you're not out trying to save the world while your own family is in some sort of need. Often times, family is where your initial ministry will start. Do you treat your brother as a man of God? Do you respect your parents? How do you serve your grandparents? How do you interact with close family friends? It's all a training ground for things to come at a later time in your life. Consequently, make this time count now so that when the moment comes, you'll be ready to activate everything you learned from fellowshipping with family. Furthermore, you'll be comfortable with making time for what's important.

Let's Break it Down:

How: Making time for what's important can be a difficult task if you are not used to doing it. At times, it may require you to decline something that you would ordinarily agree to doing. Don't let the fear of missing out hold you captive. Believe that God will honor your decision to put family first, and the reward will be greater than you thought. The best way to decide how you will make time for what's important is to first decide what exactly is important. Determine the non-negotiables in your family life. Then, when a situation presents itself, you can automatically decide how you will answer after weighing it against your non-negotiables. Another way to determine how you should prioritize your life is by looking at everything you are required to do. After that, look at a list of everything else. Take this list before God and ask Him how it should be rearranged.

What: Determining what's important will be based on your current lifestyle and who is in your life. Obviously, your child(ren) will be at the top of your list of important things. You may want to include attending extracurricular activities such as basketball, cheer, etc. Perhaps there are special performances at the school or parent functions that you would consider important. If you have extended family nearby, maybe they like to meet weekly for a large dinner gathering or brunch after church. Unfortunately, because we are only one person able to only be in one place at a time, it is impossible to think that you can be available for every function, dinner, or special moment. The idea here is to determine what you will absolutely not miss, and then plan how you will make time in your life specifically for these things.

Where: Being with family and making time for what is important can land you anywhere. That's the great part about it! I've ended up in cabins way up in the mountains and in large beautiful estates all because I learned to make time for what is important to me. It will often require a mindset change before you can really enjoy making time for what is important. Accept the fact that you are lovely and a joy to be around. Your family (no matter how incomplete you think it is) is beautiful and worthy of others' time. In fact, you and your family have something to offer those around you. Decide to let go of the negatives you've believed about yourself and your family, and open yourself up to what's really important. There's no telling where you might find yourself when you begin to think of all the blessings that can come with making time for family and what's really important in your life.

When: You must decide when you will make time. If you work a full time job, it may be necessary for you to take time off to be available for certain things. At one point, I used to miss everything that was going on at my daughter's school because of work. I thought it didn't bother her. Then, one day she was very sad and asked me why I wasn't there. We talked, and then we made an agreement that she would always tell me if there was an event that she wanted me to attend. I agreed that I would make the biggest effort to be there. From that day forward, I have not missed any event that she said she wanted me to attend. Whether it has been in the morning or in the middle of the day, I have always managed to be able to work it out to be there. Likewise, you must know that God is in your corner and wants you to be there for the important things just as much as you want to be there. Trust that He will work out the details to make it come together. If your job gives you a hard time, pray and ask God to soften the hearts of your supervisors or open doors for a job that will give you the grace to make time for what's important for your family. Remember that God cares about your family.

Why: Right now, it may seem to you that your family is incomplete. You are a single mom. Maybe you are estranged from your own parents, or you may be afraid to let new people into your life. It may seem that this is the hardest time you've ever had in your life - and maybe it is. Still, remember that your family needs you. They need you to be present and available. They need to see that you care, and they need your actions and your words to line up. When life gets tough, it is your family that will surround you with love and care. That is the way God designed family to operate. Whether it's church family, immediate family, extended family, or adopted family, treat family like family and make the most of the time you have with them.

Let's Connect it to Scripture:

♥ Romans 8:28 – "And we know that God causes everything to work together for the good of those who love God and are called according to His purpose for them."
♥ Exodus 20:12 – "Honor your father and mother. Then you will live a long, full life in the land the Lord your God is giving you."
♥ 1 Timothy 5:8 – "But those who won't care for their relatives, especially those in their own household, have denied the true faith. Such people are worse than unbelievers."
♥ Hebrews 10:24-25 - "Let us think of ways to motivate one another to acts of love and good works. And let us not neglect our meeting together, as some people do, but encourage one another, especially now that the day of His return is drawing near."

Make Time For What's Important

Let's Walk it Out:

Discovering what's important in your life is exciting. Here's to no more feeling obligated to always say yes! You are free to make choices that are good for you and your family. What's one thing that you have been missing out on that you would like to make time for because it's important to you? Write that important thing below, and include how you plan to make time for it:

_____

_____

_____

_____

_____

_____

Sign _____

Date _____

Let's Write it Out:

1. What have today's scriptures revealed to you about who God is?

2. What has been the hardest part of making time for what's important in your life and why? Take a minute to pray about this one thing and ask God for His help in overcoming whatever is holding you back.

Let's Pray it Out:

Lord, this is such a difficult task for me. Many times, I feel pulled in so many directions all at once that I'm not sure which way to go. Please help me make choices that will honor you and not hurt my family. I love my family, and it is my desire that I am present for them. Show me how to make time for what is important, and give me the ability to say no when I need to without feeling guilty. Amen.

Day Eight

Learn to Prioritize

Now, that you're a wiz at making time for what's important, it's time to get down to the nitty gritty, the meat and potatoes. Learning to prioritize is the next step! It was important to cover making time for family first, because one can easily be great at prioritizing but still miss the mark when it comes to the home front. Unless you were a professional juggler before you became a mom, learning to prioritize is essential for you. Seriously though, as a single mom you're already juggling anyway. Learning to prioritize just helps you to juggle efficiently without dropping anything.

While some people hate lists, I actually love them. (You're probably wondering who in their right mind loves lists. Well, I do! No really, I do.) Now, I know that everybody doesn't embrace the joy of list-making the way I do, and that's ok. I can grudgingly agree that list-making isn't for everybody. For arguments sake, let's just imagine that you have tons of things to do and you don't make a list. How do you remember what needs to be done and when? I'm not trying to get you to crossover into the land of list-making. I'm just trying to help you determine how you will prioritize your to-do list. For me, the list is more than just fun to write. I'll admit that if I don't write things down, I'll seriously forget what all I need to do. Perhaps your brain works a little better than mine in the memory department. If that's the case then take my word for it and treasure it, please! We all have shortcomings, and one of mine just happens to be my tendency to be forgetful. Therefore, my to-do lists are a big help when my memory decides to take a day off.

If you're not a list maker, maybe you love technology and would enjoy using some sort of list app or voice memos. One thing I know to be true is that getting your tasks out of your mind and onto a piece of paper, chalkboard, or electronic device is essential. What makes it even better is when you learn to connect with God to prioritize that list. Asking God to help you prioritize the things you need to do will ensure that you walk in a harmonious rhythm where you and God work together, instead of you working against His plans for you. If you already have some sort of method for prioritizing but you still find yourself forgetting things or missing deadlines, it may be that you're not working with God or that you're prioritizing system could use some tweaking. It may seem weird to include God in something so simple as your to-do list, but He wants to be included in every part of your life. He knows that you have things to do, and He wants to help you do it efficiently. Find peace in knowing that His grace will cover the areas where you may fall short. Prioritizing with Him ensures you a victory every time.

Let's Break it Down:

How: I will share the way that is most familiar to me. I encourage you to play around with it, as well as, pray about it to determine the best method for you. Begin by creating a list. You can create just one list or get real fancy and make several lists broken down into categories. For example, you could have a bill list with due dates to keep you on top of when to pay what. Even better, for bills you could set up an auto-pay system through your bank and never miss a payment or never have to remember one at all. Just be sure that you always have the money in your account to cover everything.

You could also create a lists of your children's activities with dates and times. In addition, you could create a list to keep track of when you will grocery shop, what you need to buy, and how much you plan to spend. Regardless of how you decide to create your list, the idea is to put those things that must be done first towards the top and the things that you have time to take care of towards the bottom of the list. For instance, if you have car maintenance due next month, but the electric bill is due in two weeks, then the car maintenance would go at the bottom of the list. Making your list this way ensures that you don't get overwhelmed with too much to do all at once. It will also help you to focus on things that currently need your attention.

What: Making a list should become a regular part of your life. Once you get more comfortable with doing so, you could expand lists to cover your goals and plans for the future. Tasks and plans are much more doable when they are written out in small steps. When determining what needs to be prioritized, don't get too caught up in what's right and what's wrong. Just be sure to cover the basics, such as your finances and anything that would turn into a consequence if you forgot all about it. Beyond that, you can decide to prioritize day by day for routine things, such as work, Facetime, kids' activities and naptimes, and grocery store runs, etc. Then, for events and other things that are monthly commitments, create a list dedicated only to those things. Be committed to actually following the list and keeping track of what gets completed or not.

Where: Prioritize wherever you'd like. There's no rule that says you have to be sitting at your kitchen table prioritizing while the kids are asleep. Just make sure you do it in a way that makes you comfortable. There are several different places that you can keep your list. There is an overabundance of apps, an Outlook or Google calendar, and even the old fashioned day planner. Wherever you decide to keep your lists, try to make it a medium that will be easily accessible for you to make quick changes or additions within arm's reach.

When: You can decide when you should prioritize based on your lifestyle. If you only have three pressing things to take care of, it may be easy to quickly arrange them in your head. However, if the day, week, or month is unusually hectic and you've got a laundry list instead of a tiny checklist, then you may want to consider prioritizing to make sure you get everything done by your scheduled deadlines. Another thing to think about is being prepared to make changes to your list. There will be times when things will happen that require some tweaking to your list. It's important that you are able to identify the changes and promptly make the necessary adjustments to your list.

Why: As much as you like to think that you are superwoman, you're just not. None of us are. Don't get me wrong - you are amazing. Prioritizing just makes you even more amazing. Once you embrace the skill, you will find time in your day that you didn't realize you even had. You will be able to sleep at night without millions of tasks running through your mind. This peace will be possible because you have it written down, you have a plan, and you have God and His grace to sustain you through it all.

Let's Connect it to Scripture:

♥ Philippians 4:13 – "For I can do everything through Christ, who gives me strength."
♥ Corinthians 12:9 – "Each time, He said, 'My grace is all you need. My power works best in weakness.' So now I am glad to boast about my weaknesses, so that the power of Christ can work through me."

♥ Psalm 143:10 – "Teach me to do your will, for you are my God! Let your good spirit lead me on level ground!"
♥ Proverbs 16:3 – "Commit your work to the Lord and your plans will be established."

Let's Walk it Out:

Now that I've gotten you super excited about using lists to prioritize, it's time to give some thought to the method you prefer to use for making your lists. Remember, it doesn't have to be the traditional pen and paper method. It just has to be effective for you. Use the lines below to write what method you've decided to use and which list you will create first.

_____

_____

_____

_____

_____

_____

Sign _____

Date _____

Learn to Prioritize

Let's Write it Out:

1. What have today's scriptures revealed to you about who God is?

2. How do you feel learning to prioritize will better benefit your life?

3. How do you think God's grace will help you be more efficient when prioritizing your time and commitments?

Let's Pray it Out:

Heavenly Father, thank you for providing your grace, which is enough for me. I pray that you would help me to prioritize my time and commitments wisely. I understand that you long to be a part of every detail of my life. Forgive me for leaving you out of certain areas of my life. I surrender my day-to-day activities to you, Lord. I ask that you would guide me every step of the way. Amen.

Day Nine

Pray, Pray, Pray

I love prayer! Seriously, I think it's so amazing because it packs power. Growing up in church, I used to watch in amazement as the older members prayed so effortlessly. I always thought to myself that there was no way I could pray like that. Then, as I got older and more involved in church, I began to wonder what prayer was all about. I even attempted to pray the way I had seen before. Although it felt right, I wasn't sure if it was right. I wondered if the most effective prayers were the really strong and passionate ones like I witnessed as a child. I even wondered if only people who called themselves intercessors or prayer warriors saw their prayers get answered. Unfortunately, there was a time when I felt as if I lacked the praying gift. As a result, I kind of wrote off prayer. I said the meal blessing most of us grew up learning and that was about it. It wasn't until I had a crisis that I really came back to prayer. (Isn't that how it usually is? We don't pray regularly. We only do it when we think we need help. The problem is we always need help - even when we think we don't need it.)

I spent eight years in the Navy, and my active duty time came to an abrupt end during the last year of service. I didn't see it coming, and in no way was I prepared for it. However, God had a plan. After I was discharged, I spent the next seven months unemployed. That was the first time I had been jobless in eight years! While it was a freeing experience, it was also very scary. I was in a position I had never been in before. I was collecting unemployment compensation, and it was not nearly enough. Therefore, I started to pray and tell God what I needed. I didn't use any fancy words or spend hours balling my eyes out. I just expressed how worried I was and that I needed money for specific necessities. Honestly, I didn't really know what would happen after I prayed, but I was desperate. I had nowhere to turn. However, I remembered from growing up in church that prayer was something that I could do.

Well, God showed up in a big way, and I began to praise Him in song and dance. The more I praised, the more I was drawn to Him. I was so thankful that He answered my prayers. Sometimes it was a little nerve-wracking because a bill would be due, and I didn't have the money. However, right at that last moment, I'd miraculously have the money. During that entire seven months of unemployment, He never once let me down. I was so blessed that I would go to the grocery store, and people would randomly buy my groceries. In addition, I'd have a friend who needed a babysitter, and she would insist on paying me for helping her out right at a time when my gas tank was on empty. I'll never forget that season with God. It was then that I learned that God hears me, He loves me, and He has always taken care of me.

I hope that I have your attention about increasing your prayer life. When you pray, it's also a good habit to write your prayers down with dates. That will help you keep track of every prayer that you have ever uttered - big or small. Then, when God answers your prayer, go back and put down how He answered it and when. As you see God move on your behalf, your connection with Him will get deeper. Moreover, you will have a desire to press in with prayer even more. You don't have to be all fancy with God. He is your Father so talk to Him like the perfect Dad He is. Prayer is one little thing that has power that can go beyond what you could ever imagine.

Let's' Break it Down:

How: Several books cover the power of prayer. I encourage you to explore them as you get more comfortable with praying. For now, let's stick to the basics in prayer. From church, I learned a very simple acronym (ACTS) to explain how to pray. The first step is to **A**dore. Here, you want to spend some time focusing your heart and attention on God by showing Him some love and respect. Declare God's character based off Bible verses and praise and worship songs. If you don't know where to start, use the alphabet by saying something like, "God you are awesome. God you are beautiful. God you are caring…"

From there, prayer flows into **C**onfessing. Take time to confess your sins and shortcomings. Ask the Holy Spirit to search your heart and reveal areas that need to be confessed and changed. The next step is to **T**hank. Think of the many ways God has blessed you, and begin to thank Him for them. After that, you will need to **S**eek. During this time of prayer, you are asking God for His help in your life. This is also the time to bring before Him the needs of others near and far. Remember to take your time during prayer. You are literally having a conversation with God.

Pray, Pray, Pray

What: Because God knows all, there isn't anything that you could bring up in prayer that would be a surprise to Him. His desire is for us to become mature Christians. Much like when your child wants something and you want to teach them how to verbally ask for it instead of just grunting and pointing, God wants us to open our mouths and talk to Him. He wants to know that we want Him to be an active part of our lives. So, talk about whatever you want with God. He is literally the safest person ever to talk to about anything. Another thing is to remember that the Bible is the sword of the Spirit. It is our only defensive weapon. Take that knowledge into your prayers and start speaking Scripture over people and circumstances. Then, watch your prayers turn into a fierce weapon. This is an elevated level of prayer, but you can do it. Just let the Holy Spirit lead you.

Where: Pray anywhere! I used to think that I could only pray when it was quiet and I was completely alone. If you wait for the times in your day when you're actually alone in complete silence, it would put a major damper on your prayer life. Because prayer is simply talking to God, it can happen anywhere - regardless of who is around. Not every prayer needs to be fifteen minutes long either. Sometimes it's a one-minute talk, or maybe you just have a question. You could be driving and realize you are lost. At that moment, just ask God to direct you in the right path. Maybe you just got a call while at work that a friend has gone into labor early. You could send up a quick prayer that everything will be alright with her and the baby. Don't ever feel like there's some sort of custom when it comes to prayer. Whenever there's a need, pray. Whether you're driving, at the movies, or out to eat, it doesn't matter. Your eyes don't have to be closed, your head doesn't have to be bowed down, and your hands don't have to be clasped. All that is required is that your heart is in right standing before God.

When: Some people have grown up thinking that prayer means only praying in the morning, praying whenever you eat, and praying at night. This is just not true. You can pray whenever. It is not necessary that you only pray at a certain time of the day or only when you need help. Because praying is just talking to God, you could pray just to give thanks or you could pray and ask for God to keep you from losing it on a rude co-worker. It truly doesn't matter when you pray, just pray often.

Why: Prayer is an open line of communication between you and God. How blessed we are to have God available to us at all times! Don't turn it into a religious obligation. Instead, use prayer as a way to build a beautiful relationship with Him. You will have a hard time seeing God move in your life if you subject Him to an obligation.

Let's Connect it to Scripture:

♥ Matthew 6:6 – "But when you pray, go away by yourself, shut the door behind you, and pray to your Father in private. Then your Father, who sees everything will reward you."
♥ Mark 11:25 – "But when you are praying, first forgive anyone you are holding a grudge against, so that your Father will forgive your sins, too."
♥ Philippians 4:6 – "Don't worry about anything; instead pray about everything. Tell God what you need and thank Him for all He has done."
♥ John 15:7 – "But if you remain in me and my words remain in you, you may ask for anything you want and it will be granted."

Let's Walk it Out:

Prayer is such a beautiful thing. I hope that you will come to experience it in a way that draws your heart closer to God. What is a custom you grew up believing about prayer that you have learned is not true? What truth about prayer can you replace that custom with?

_____

_____

_____

_____

_____

_____

Sign _____

Date _____

Pray, Pray, Pray

Let's Write it Out:

1. What have today's scriptures revealed to you about who God is?

2. What is something that you never thought to pray to God about but you are now excited to share with Him?

3. How do you plan to share the power of prayer with your kids and incorporate it into the family?

Let's Pray it Out:

Lord, I'm ready to connect with you in prayer. It is such a comfort to know that I can talk to you about anything. Help me to break off wrong ideas about what prayer is so that I can be free to experience power in my prayer time with you. I pray that I will be able to take what I learn from you and pass it on to my children. Amen.

Day Ten

Learn to Fight

I was not a fighter growing up. Actually, I was very quiet and timid. I rarely spoke directly to anyone, and I usually hid behind my mother during interactions with others. I'll admit that while I wish that everything had just switched for me in a moment, it did not happen this way. It took me a while to overcome my shyness, and it was not easy. In fact, a series of God-orchestrated experiences over several years helped me come out of my shell. One experience in particular was when my parents put my brother and me in Taekwondo and Aikido. My brother had much more fight in him than I did, so this was a great channel of energy and aggression for him. However, for me, it was just plain scary. I didn't want to hit anyone, and I definitely didn't want to get hit either.

In one of the first few sessions, I remember feeling very nervous about the fact that we had to spar with each other. I kept thinking, *"Wait, we have to really hit each other?"* I could feel fear boiling up in my stomach from the mere anticipation that I was going to have to hit someone or even worse get hit at some point. Now, this was not MMA fighting. We had plenty of pads on, and we were fully clothed in our Taekwondo dobok or uniform. Still, it just didn't seem right to me. On top of that, they broke the news that we would compete in tournaments and break pieces of wood in half! About that time, I was desperately giving my mom and dad major puppy dog eyes in hopes that they had no idea what they had gotten us into. I hoped that they would grab us and run for the door. Unfortunately, I was not so lucky.

As the weeks went on, I trained and even sparred. I went to tournaments and competed against people I had never met. Yes, I was scared every time. However, at that point, I knew there was no way of getting out of it. Therefore, I tried to do my best while still being afraid. I even started breaking pieces of wood. I broke them every time with my hands and feet. Sometimes, I had to give it more than one try, but I always walked away a winner. Eventually, I figured out that all the training and sparring was not just to freak me out. It actually had a purpose. The time I spent learning to block, how to give a punch, different kicks, and how to flex the foot was all to prepare me to be successful at the tournaments. When we were all done with Taekwondo training, I may not have been a black belt, but I did know how to defend myself. Furthermore, I gained a little bit of confidence on my journey towards coming out of my shell.

I share this story with you because, as Christians, we are in a fight. I don't mean the kind of schoolyard fight where you meet your foe in the parking lot at 3 p.m. This enemy- the devil - fights dirty. He's looking for every weakness you have, and he wants to use it against you to destroy your life. He doesn't stop there; he goes after your kids, your parents, and anyone else who is not on guard against him. He will use anything made available to him to keep you so distracted, so angry, so hurt, so drunk, or so high that you miss out on the fullness of all God has for you. He will exploit you, make you feel guilty, and paralyze you with fear. He will even drive you to the point that you give up on life all together and lose the desire to step into the promises and provision of God for your life.

To fight an enemy, you must first acknowledge that you have one. This is key because so many people today do not truly believe a real devil exists. This gives the enemy free reign and access to so many people's lives without them having any defense system whatsoever. Furthermore, it causes those individuals to be big, vulnerable targets to the enemy. Rather than continue down this destructive path, it's time to wake up and fight. I wrestled with the idea of a spiritual fight. In Taekwondo, I had a hard enough time with fighting what was right in front me. When thinking about a spiritual fight, I wondered how was I supposed to fight something that's in a spiritual realm. Out of fear, I hid out for as long as I could. Then came a point when I started to get angry. I was angry at how much time I spent being exhausted by being tossed around by him. I was even angry at the drama happening in my family.

When I began to acknowledge my anger, I learned the true power of God's Word. We all have been given spiritual armor to fight the enemy. Every piece of armor serves a purpose. Out of all the armor you have, the Word is the one defensive piece. It is your weapon. It is your sword. A sword is no use if you have no idea how to yield it or if it just sits on your nightstand like a precious decoration during a battle. Your sword was made for battle. Moreover, it was made to fight the enemy for your life and for your family's life. You already have the victory, because God's plan is foolproof. Now, all you have to do is trust His plan, take out your sword, and slay in the Spirit.

Let's Break it Down:

How: Using the Bible as your mighty sword may take some practice, but remember that the Holy Spirit is there to help you as you grow into a warrior princess. To use the Word, you must know the Word. This is why your Facetime is so important. Put in the extra effort to read and commit the scriptures to memory. Accordingly, when something arises, the verse will be already in your heart and mind. Take your studies seriously and allow the Word to transform you. As you continually expose yourself to it, you will find that it changes the way you think, the way you feel, and the way you act. More importantly, you will become the person God designed you to be, and your old ways will be overcome by the light of God and His Word. When you use the Word of God to fight, it will be a mighty, strategic blow coming from your mouth. It will also be powered by the Holy Spirit as it is cutting off the enemy's attack. Speak the Words out loud with boldness, and watch God lead you to victory.

What: You must be familiar with the scriptures so that you can be effective when you fight. It is not enough to just open the bible and pick a random verse. You have to go for the verse that speaks directly to the area that the enemy is gunning for. If it is a stirring of drama in your family, you will want to speak verses over your family that encourages peace, love, and forgiveness. If it is a sickness, you will want to find verses that claim the blood of Jesus and healing in the body. If it is an attack on your finances or other provisions, you will want to find scriptures that declare the goodness of God to His children. If it is a temptation to have sex, pull out those scriptures that warn against these things. Take some time also to read Matthew 4 and learn straight from Jesus how to use Scripture to rebuke the enemy.

Where: The Bible says to always have on your armor. You must always be ready to fight. The enemy does not give you a break because you're busy or tired. Therefore, your fight could take place anywhere. It could happen in the middle of a conversation or in the form of unexpected news. Because of that, it's important that you be on guard for these situations. Remember that you are not in a fight with humans, so refrain from attacking flesh and blood. Learn to recognize the spirit that the enemy is using, and use the Word of God appropriately at that moment. To get even more guidance on using the Bible as your sword, I recommend that you read *Fervent* by Priscilla Shirer. It is a great book on strategic prayer.

When: The purpose of training is to prepare you for something. Whether it's for a race, a game, or a test, when things get real, your training should naturally take over. It is important that you train in a way that will help you to be successful when the real battle takes place. Keep that in mind as you study God's Word. When you are properly trained, no matter when the fight comes, your training will automatically kick in, and you'll be ready to win. As I said, the enemy doesn't fight fairly. He will do his best to catch you off guard. He will attack you while you're on vacation, during a church picnic, or while you're out grocery shopping. Whatever it takes to throw you off your game, he will use it as a weapon to destroy you. Remain armored in God's word, and be prepared for battle.

Why: In this life, you will always have trials, troubles, and temptations. That is why God gave us specific instructions on how to fight the good fight. He wants us to be prepared, confident, and courageous. He already gave you the victory. You just have to choose to walk in it.

Let's Connect it to Scripture:

♥ Ephesians 6:12 -17 – "For we are not fighting against flesh-and-blood enemies, but against evil rulers and authorities of the unseen world, against mighty powers in this dark world and against evil spirits in the heavenly places. Therefore, put on every piece of God's armor so you will be able to resist the enemy in the time of evil. Then after the battle you will still be standing firm. Stand your ground putting on the belt of truth and the body armor of God's righteousness. For shoes put on the peace that comes from the Good News so that you will be fully prepared. In addition to all of these, hold up the shield of faith to stop the fiery arrows of the devil. Put on salvation as your helmet and take the sword of the Spirit, which is the Word of God."
♥ 1 Peter 5:8 – "Stay alert! Watch out for your great enemy the devil. He prowls around like a roaring lion, looking for someone to devour."
Romans 8:37 – "No despite all these things, overwhelming victory is ours through Christ, who loved us."
♥ Hebrews 4:12 – "For the Word of God is alive and powerful. It is sharper than the sharpest two-edged sword, cutting between soul and spirit, between joint and marrow. It exposes our innermost thoughts and desires."

Learn to Fight

♥ Luke 10:19-20 – "Look, I have given you authority over all the power of the enemy, and you can walk among snakes and scorpions and crush them. Nothing will injure you. But don't rejoice because evil spirits obey you; rejoice because your names are registered in heaven."

Let's Walk it Out:

Now that you have the inside scoop on being fierce in battle, let's take some time to survey your grounds. Where is the devil wreaking havoc in your life? Pray and ask God to show you. On the lines below, write in which areas of your life you are ready to fight, and list one scripture you will use to shut down the enemy.

_____

_____

_____

_____

_____

_____

Sign _____

Date _____

Let's Write it Out:

1. What has today's scripture revealed to you about who God is?

2. Is there anything about today's topic that you are unclear on? If so, what? Pray and ask the Holy Spirit to give you understanding in this area. If you are a disciple or mentee, discuss this with that person.

3. How does it feel to know that the Bible is a spiritual sword and that you have been given authority to wield it and be victorious? What is one area of your life that you are excited to use your sword and experience some victory?

Let's Pray it Out:

Lord, thank you for the gift of your Holy Spirit. Thank you that I am never alone. I confess that I have been afraid of the battle. Please teach me how to fight and be victorious in you. I am tired of the enemy having free reign in my family's life and in my life. Today, I take a stand in my authority with you. Amen.

Day Eleven

Keep the Faith

This is something near and dear to my heart, and I always feel as if I can't have enough of it. I used to tell people that if I could sum up my life in just one word, it would be *faith*. Every major turning point in my life has taken major faith to conquer. While I sometimes felt alone on the journey I never stopped believing that God would bring me out. Faith of a mustard seed right? It's typical to feel alone in things like this, and I'm quite sure that there are many single moms (and others) who would agree with me. Yet, it amazes me how God continues to move in my life. That's why the story of Abraham has always intrigued me so much. Although he was very flawed, Abraham had great faith in God. So much of it in fact, that he was willing to sacrifice his own son in obedience to the Lord. It's no wonder why Abraham is the Father of Faith. It would be wise for us to take some tips from Abraham. His story can be found in Genesis 11-25. Please take some time to read it, because I know that you will be inspired by his life.

Faith is believing you'll receive something that you can't see. It may be something that you prayed for or something God showed you. Maybe God showed you a vision of something you would do one day. Yet, looking around you don't even seem anywhere close to doing that. You may think that you're not living in the right place, you don't possess the right education, or you don't know the right people. Either way, it requires you to believe even when there is no evidence that it will come to pass. You just have to know that you know that God will make it happen. I know that believing in the unseen is difficult enough, but you can't just stop there. There are so many times when we just put God in a tiny, little box with little expectations of His power. All too often, we seriously forget that we serve a living God who is all powerful and able to do the impossible. He doesn't need to stretch first or go ask for permission. He only requires that you actually believe and have faith in Him.

Reading through the Gospels of Matthew, Mark, and Luke, you will learn a lot about Jesus and His ministry. Jesus healed a lot of people. You will see in Scripture that when He healed someone, He repeatedly said, "Your faith has healed you," or "Your faith has made you well." This is evidence that faith is a big deal to Him, and it should be a big thing to you as well. In fact, it saddened Jesus to see people have such little faith. In addition to the prerequisite of having the faith of a mustard seed, you must also take action! The Bible tells us in, James 2:17 that "faith without works is dead." It's a great thing to believe God, but I want to challenge you to get your walk, your talk, and your actions lined up too.

It's much like when you first found out you were pregnant. The first thing you probably did was confirm it by going out and buying a pregnancy test. Once you got the official two lines, your next step was probably to call and make an appointment with the doctor. Because you wanted a healthy baby, I'm sure that you followed all of the doctor's recommendations. You took your prenatal vitamins, you were careful with what you ate, and you made sure not to overexert yourself. You did all of this well before you could hear your baby's heartbeat, feel it moving, or see your belly growing out. You did this because you believed (faith) that you were pregnant and wanted to do everything possible to ensure a successful pregnancy and birth. You must do the same with faith and action. When you are believing for something God shared with you or that you prayed about, you cannot just believe it and then continue life as usual. You need to listen for direction from God, and then you need to WALK in that direction. Just like you nurtured your baby in your belly until it was born, you also need to nurture that seed of faith until it is time to birth it.

Let's Break it Down:

How: We all have faith - some just in lesser or greater amounts. If you feel that you are low in faith, I would encourage you to ask God to give you more. After making your request known to God, be prepared for a shift in your life because you will not be able to grow in your comfort zone. Usually, the building up of faith requires being in some sort of bumpy place financially, emotionally, or physically. So be thankful anytime you must operate uncomfortably, because that means that God wants you to grow. Let's begin to have faith in God. Believe that He is all that He says He is, and believe that He has a magnificent plan for your life.

What: Being a Christian is an act of faith. You must believe that Jesus died on the cross and rose from the grave. Faith is the cornerstone of our lives as believers. Therefore, it should carry over into all we do. If you have faith that Jesus is your Savior, then why would you not believe that He has a good plan for your life? Remember that faith and action go together. When you're believing for something be sure to act on it - even if it is baby steps. If you are believing God for a new job, make sure your resume is updated, that you have practiced your interview skills, and that you have business clothes prepared. If you're really believing God for a job, you would want to be prepared for that job and looking for opportunities. You never know how God may present the new job to you. If you are believing God for a Godly husband, it would be wise for you to prepare yourself to be a Godly wife. Read books, interact with Christian married women, go to relationship conferences, take care of your debt, and learn how to cook. Be sure that you'll be ready when God sends your husband in your direction.

When: I once heard the saying that "preparation is another form of expectation." (Can I get an amen on that?!) You wouldn't waste time preparing for what you do not expect. Why would you buy healthy foods and a gym membership if you do not expect to lose weight and live a healthier lifestyle? Why would you put money away in a savings account if you don't expect to build a nest egg for your family and yourself? We should always live in joyful expectation of the good things Father God has for us. With joyful expectation comes necessary preparation. You could be holding yourself back from receiving God's blessings in your life. If you are not prepared, how can He give you a gift you are not ready to receive? Do not wait until tomorrow to decide what you will believe. Believe God and take your first baby step now.

Where: Every area of our lives requires us to faith. I have faith in God that He will provide for my family, that He will help me parent my daughter, and that He will forgive me of my sins and throw them into the sea of forgetfulness when I confess them to Him. One way to stretch your faith is to start looking for how much faith is required in your life. I'm sure that once you do this, you will see that you have more faith than you thought. Is there a new career that you feel like God is calling you into but you're terrified to make the transition? Have you been feeling convicted in your heart to start tithing your 10%? Is there a conference that you feel you should attend, but are afraid to go? Take some advice that I once was told: "Go to the edge of the cliff, swan dive off, and know that the hand of God is beneath you." When you're walking on the water with Jesus, the wind and tide are bound to come. Keep your focus on Jesus, even if everything around you is not looking good.

Have faith that He will never steer you wrong. Your best life will always be found beside Him. Have faith in that.

Why: Faith is a requirement by God. It is that simple.

Let's Connect it to Scripture:

♥ Genesis 15:6 – "And Abram believed the Lord, and the Lord counted him as righteous because of his faith."
♥ Matthew 17:20 - "You don't have enough faith," Jesus told them. "I tell you the truth, if you had faith even as small as a mustard seed, you could say to this mountain, 'Move from here to there,' and it would move. Nothing would be impossible."
♥ James 2:17 – "So you see, faith by itself isn't enough. Unless it produces good deeds, it is dead and useless."
Romans 3:22 – "We are made right with God by placing our faith in Jesus Christ. And this is true for everyone who believes, no matter who we are."
♥ Hebrews 11:6 – "And it is impossible to please God without faith. Anyone who wants to come to Him must believe that God exists and that He rewards those who sincerely seek Him."

Let's Walk it Out:

Since faith is a requirement by God, I don't want you to go any further in this book without enacting it. If you are lacking faith in your life, I want you to put this book down and put your pride aside. Stop right now and tell God that you want more faith. Then, sit and wait to hear His response to you. Write the response below.

_____

_____

_____

_____

_____

_____

Sign _____

Date _____

Keep the Faith

Let's Write it Out:

1. What have today's scriptures reveal to you about who God is?

2. In what area of your life are you currently lacking faith? Why?

3. Did you read Abraham's story? Is there something that you've done that you feel disqualifies you from being blessed by God? Why? Pray, ask for forgiveness, know that you are forgiven, and take a baby step in the direction God shows you.

Let's Pray it Out:

Father in Heaven, your ways are just and righteous. Please forgive me for putting limitations on you in my life with my lack of faith. Thank you for even allowing faith the size of a mustard seed to honor you. Lord, I pray and ask that you would increase my faith. Let it move me into action that I may see your goodness in my life. Amen.

Day Twelve

Watch Your Mouth

Did your mom ever make you wash your mouth out with soap when you got too sassy? I know there were a few times I experienced a soapy mouth. Let's not even discuss those times when soap was not available, and it was a thump to the mouth instead. Well, needless to say, most of us are still walking around with those same childish mouths. Before those of you who struggle with foul language start feeling guilty, let me say that this topic is not just for you. This topic is also for those who have an issue with negativity, down talk, and discouragement. You are not alone here. Being in the military for many years, I had picked up the very bad habit of using curse words regularly. When God really showed me what I looked like using all those obscenities, I was appalled. It was not at all how I wanted to look (especially as a mother) or how I wanted God to see me. I almost immediately stopped using those words. However, for years after that, I struggled with something just as bad. What's worse is that I never realized it was a problem or how it impacted my life until a lot of damage had already been done.

I walked around always saying what I couldn't do. I can't write a book. I can't find a good man. I can't get out of debt. As a result, that is exactly what happened. I would say that I'd never feel good about myself. I'd never make any friends. I'd never be able to grow out my hair. Meanwhile, for all the years that I walked around saying those things, I never experienced breakthrough in those areas. I literally spoke those negative things into existence. As a child, I never truly understood what it meant. I honestly thought it was one of those catchy things old people said to each other in passing. Looking back, I can see that I literally released those negative things into my life when I spoke them constantly. This happened because whatever we say or think about is what we begin to do. This revolving evolution then affects every action taken going forward. We'll discuss this more in the next chapter.

When I realized that my words were paralyzing growth in many areas of my life, I was determined to change that immediately. Why was I even saying that I couldn't get out of debt or that I couldn't find a good man? I actually really wanted to get out of debt and have a good man in my life. Did I believe that I was money savvy enough to get all my bills paid off? Did I believe that I was worthy to have a good man in my life? Well, if I really believed it, then I had to start speaking it. This part may take some reprogramming, but you can surely rid yourself of the negative self-talk. If you are anything like me, you've been talking this way for a while and may be doing it without even realizing it. Still, just because you've been this way for a while, it does not mean you are beyond the hope of change. Jesus died so that you may have life and have it to the fullest. Don't let your speech steal away your God-given inheritance.

Let's Break it Down:

How: Remember that we learned that the Word is very powerful. One sure way to change your speech is to find some verses that would speak life into an area that you have been speaking death. I would encourage you to choose at least one scripture for your particular area of struggle, and commit it to memory. Then, whenever you find yourself about to say a curse word or about put yourself down, say that scripture instead. This is not a quick fix, but stay persistent, and I promise you will see victory in that area of your life. After that, you can feel confident enough to attack the next area of your life with scripture in the same way.

What: Deciding what to say all depends on your struggle. If you are struggling with using foul language, then you would want to find a scripture that specifically deals with the type of words you should be using when you talk. If you are having issues with not feeling pretty, it would be helpful to search for verses that cover how precious you are to God. Your talk reveals what is in your heart. Therefore, to counteract ugly talk of any kind, give it a bath in its exact opposite found in the Word.

Where: If you're like most people, you are probably talking most of the day. You're talking to yourself, talking to other people, talking in meetings, and talking on the phone. It's actually amazing how much of our day we spend talking. Thus, it is not just the words you speak to yourself that must be corrected, but also the words that you speak to others. Are you overly sarcastic, rude, or condescending? These things do not honor God, and this is not the way that He intended us to speak to each other. Therefore, as you work on checking the way that you talk to yourself, remember to be mindful of how you speak to others as well.

When: Since your words have the power to affect the outcome of your life, it is important to bridle what is ineffective immediately. Neither you, your children, nor the people who God needs you to speak to can afford for you to drag your feet on watching your mouth. Start today. There is no need to wait. You receive no benefit from putting it off. If you feel overwhelmed in this area, that's okay. Just choose the most pressing area of your words that needs work and start there. There is no reason to take on a full overhaul of your speech in a day. Now, this is not to say that God may not do that for you. If He does, give Him some praise! However, He may need you to journey through this process little by little, and that's okay, too. No matter how He decides to walk alongside you during this process, never stop giving Him praise.

Why: God hears all. Knowing this should be enough for you to pay more attention to what you say. Not only that, but we will all have to explain the nonsense we spoke on judgement day. Because we are saved, we are fully forgiven for our silly talk. Nevertheless, wouldn't it be nice to keep that list as short as possible. Outside of that, you will never be a ready vessel for God to use if you are not a good steward over your mouth. Blessings and curses cannot come from the same mouth. So, decide how you want to be seen by others. Most importantly, decide how you want God to see you, and then make the change.

Let's Connect it to Scripture:

♥ Proverbs 18:21 – "The tongue can bring life or death; those who love to talk will reap the consequences."
♥ James 1:19 – "Understand this, my dear brothers and sisters: You must all be quick to listen, slow to speak and slow to get angry."
♥ Ephesians 4:29 – "Don't use foul or abusive language. Let everything you say be good and helpful, so that your words will be an encouragement to those who hear them."
♥ Colossians 4:6 – "Let your conversation be gracious and attractive so that you will have the right response for everyone."
♥ Matthew 12:36 – "And I tell you this, you must give an account on judge-

ment day for every idle word you speak."

Let's Walk it Out:

Understanding the power of what we say is revelatory. Take a moment and ask God to reveal to you an area or thing that you constantly say that is debilitating His work in your life. Then, ask Him for a Scripture that you can say instead. Write what God says below and commit to working on it immediately.

_____

_____

_____

_____

_____

_____

Sign _____

Date _____

Watch Your Mouth

Let's Write it Out:

1. What did today's scriptures reveal to you about who God is?

2. How have the things you say to yourself affected who you are and what you do in life?

3. What is one way that you can use your words to build up your children and not tear them down? (Even while they're babies, you can speak life over your children. Start early)

Let's Pray it Out:

Lord, you are so loving and kind to me. You are always ready to help and encourage me to greatness. Forgive me for allowing my speech to control me and dishonor you. Thank you that your Word is alive, powerful, and available to me so that I can change the way I use my words. It is my desire to use my words for life and not death. I ask that you would help me to put your Word in my heart and change my speech. Amen.

Day Thirteen

Think God Thoughts

Thinking good thoughts is a power move for your life. Did you know that your thoughts can and will dictate your actions? This is why the enemy loves to mess with your head. It's an isolated place. He can create another world within your mind that no one else is even aware exists. He does this by infiltrating your thoughts. If this is new to you, then you may not be aware of how devastating this type of trickery is to your life. He will place lies in your head and give you fearful thoughts, lustful thoughts, and bad ideas. Even worse, if you are not aware of this scheme, he can easily have you thinking that these are truly your own thoughts. Please realize that you have the power given to you by Christ to take authority over your thoughts. In the words of Joyce Meyer, "the mind is a battlefield" that requires courage and boldness. It requires an armored soldier ready for war to take possession of their land. In this case, you are the soldier and your mind is your land that you must fight to possess. The enemy can often be relentless in this area. This is why people may struggle with depression, suicide, and other mental issues.

Jesus did not come to Earth in human form, live a poor man's life, and then die on a cross for our sins (not His own) so that we could go through this life strangled by the enemy's attacks on our mind. He did this so that we would be victorious over all of the enemy's schemes. The best way to attain victory is to know your enemy and to know how he operates. There's an old saying, "The devil ain't got no new tricks." I used to always laugh when I heard it. Then, I really thought about it, and I noticed how the enemy continually causes ruckus in my life using very similar attacks. Once I was able to recognize them, I was more prepared to resist them.

This is why it is so important to spend time with God daily and to stay in the Word. When your mind is saturated with God's powerful Word, it makes it much more difficult for the enemy to come at you with something crazy. This is because you will immediately recognize it and render him powerless over you. The truth is he is powerless over you already. You are the daughter of the Mighty King. Therefore, the devil can't touch you. If you put your guard down and become complacent, you leave a door open for him to creep into your mind. While the mental fight with the enemy can be tiresome, don't you dare grow weary or fearful. Your life and the life of your children depends on you taking that power and using your authority to knock down strongholds.

Let's Break it Down:

How: Thinking good (God) thoughts requires a physical action, even though it is a mental function. You have to physically determine that the enemy is giving you a thought that isn't yours. Then, you have to call it the lie that it is! Say it out loud if necessary, but let the devil know you mean business. After that, take that thought and rebuke it with the Word of God. I've been covering using scripture in your daily life because I truly believe it helps us to be strong, mature Christians. So, again use verses to counteract the enemy's attacks on your thoughts.

What: In order to know how to manage your thought life, you must know what is from God and what isn't. Moreover, you must be able to recognize the character of God. This comes through spending time with Him and His Word. As a result, when you get a thought, you can test it against God's Word. Remember, God never changes, so don't be thrown off by something that is close to His Word. The devil is very clever at sending you counterfeits that'll be so close to the real thing that if you aren't on you're A-game, you will totally miss it. If it's not 1000% aligned with God's Word, don't you dare keep that thought. Don't play around with it or even meditate on it. Instead, throw it back immediately, and then diffuse it with what God really says.

Where: The internal fight will always take place in the mind. You should even be careful for thoughts that other people will try to give you. This is another clever tactic that the enemy uses. If he cannot infiltrate your mind directly, then he will use your close friends or family to try to put debilitating thoughts into your head. Love your family, but recognize when the enemy is up to his dirty work. Remember, he uses anything he can to bring you down. That is also true for media or cultural standards. The media and culture today both have a very strong influence on people's thoughts and actions. Therefore, I encourage you to be careful what you watch and put little stock into media personas, information, and advertisement. The world is a dark place, and almost everything we encounter is influenced by the enemy. Don't forget the enemy's ability to use these things to put crazy thoughts into your head.

When: Our minds are bombarded with thoughts non-stop throughout the day. It has been said that an inactive mind can be the devil's playground. Consequently, purpose to keep your mind active and choose wisely how you will do that. These could be simple things like talking to God throughout your day, listening to praise and worship music, or meditating on a particular verse. Don't let your mind go idle. Keep it focused on the things of God, and the enemy will have a hard time taking over your thoughts.

Why: How you choose to think about yourself and your life (past and present) will overflow into every aspect of what you do or don't do. This includes spilling over into your children and affecting their growth and potential. It is not always an easy task to conquer, but it is not impossible. Once you start working on thinking differently, though, you will easily begin to feel the difference. It is so freeing when the chains in your mind are loosed in Jesus's name. There are so many ways that God wants to show up and show out in your life. However, the enemy can give you a mindset that will stop you from starting that business, making a new friend, or attending a conference. Do not let a mindset planted by the enemy have you believing that you aren't good enough. As a child of God, you have permission to give back anything that is not from God.

Let's Connect it to Scripture:

♥ 2 Timothy 1:7 – "For God has not given us a spirit of fear and timidity, but of power, love and self-discipline (sound mind)."
♥ 1 Peter 5:8 – "Stay alert! Watch out for your great enemy the devil. He prowls around like a roaring lion looking for someone to devour."
♥ Ephesians 6:11 – "Put on all of God's armor so that you will be able to stand firm against all strategies of the devil."
♥ 2 Corinthians 10:5 – "We destroy every proud obstacle that keeps people from knowing God. We capture their rebellious thoughts and teach them to obey Christ."

♥ Philippians 4:8 – "And now, dear brothers and sisters, one final thing. Fix your thoughts on what is true, and honorable, and right, and pure and lovely, and admirable. Think about things that are excellent and worthy of praise."

♥Colossians 3:2 – "Think about the things of Heaven, not the things of Earth."

Let's Walk it Out:

It's time to get free! What's one thought that you've struggled with for a long time? Why do you think the enemy has bombarded you with this thought? Write the answer below, and then pray and ask God to reveal the truth found in His Word to replace that thought (lie).

_____

_____

_____

_____

_____

_____

Sign _____

Date _____

Let's Write it Out:

1. What have today's scriptures revealed to you about who God is?

2. What is one way you can keep your mind active and focused on the things of God?

Let's Pray it Out:

Lord, I am so fascinated by your overflowing love and how much you care for me. Forgive me for letting the enemy control my thoughts. Thank you for leaving your Word and Holy Spirit to help guide me. I pray that I would learn to focus my mind on you. Teach me to recognize the enemy's tactics. Give me boldness to use my authority to take every thought captive so that I may be victorious in Jesus's name. Amen.

Day Fourteen

Make Room for Expectancy

I really do not like clutter. Clutter can make a room that's full of potential and life feel like the oxygen is being sucked right out of it. It creates a lifeless space and leaves little room for anything new. Even more than that, it's difficult to know what's in a cluttered room, what is needed, and what is no longer useful. In many ways, our lives can often become like a cluttered room. This clutter is not always a physical thing. It can also be financial, spiritual or relationship based. Regardless, it is important to first identify it, and then get organized. In actuality, external clutter always mirrors some type of internal clutter. Although clutter will constantly come up in your life you can have control over it so that it doesn't keep you from growing.

Some people believe that organization is a special gift. My daughter is one of these people. Her bedroom used to be atrocious. She was not doing a good job of keeping it tidy at all. It was cluttered for sure. Even worse is that she looked at organization as some type of mean chore. I had given her speech after speech and lecture after lecture, and still there was no change. Finally, I asked her what would make her room an enjoyable place that she would want to keep clean. She gave me a wish list of colors and designs that she liked. I shared with her that she could have the room she wanted, but first she had to clean out the clutter to make room for the new things. She quickly went about throwing out and organizing everything in her room. She was even beginning to enjoy it as she saw how great her room was looking. She was literally making room for expectancy.

Eventually her room was nice and tidy. The clutter was gone. Anything that was not needed had been removed, and everything else had been well-organized. We went to the store and got the things that she needed to create the look that she wanted, and soon her room was complete. Had she not removed the clutter, she would have never created the space for the room that she really wanted. She had to learn how to let go of old things in order to make room for new and better things. This is the core of making room for expectancy. This is what you have to do in your lives. You have to be willing to let go of the clutter in your life to make room for other things. Let go of the old mindsets, old clothes, and old ways of doing things. Release the clutter to make room for something new and better in your life. Sometimes, expectancy doesn't have anything to do with what you want to bring into your life. Sometimes it is all about what God wants to bring into your life. If you're battling old mindsets, bad habits, and activities that are no longer functional, then you are cluttering your life with things that could be blocking you from receiving God's best in your life.

Let's Break it Down:

How: Releasing clutter can be a process, especially for those who have a difficult time letting go of things. First, determine what you want to make room for. Is it a new couch, a future husband, a business, or a friendship? Once you know what you need to make room for, it's time to discover the clutter in that area of your life that needs to be cleaned out. For example, I deeply desired a husband and prayed on it (repeatedly) with expectation that God would bring him into my life at the right time. In my expectation of this happening, the Holy Spirit gave me a revelation. How was God going to bring a good man into my life when I was still holding on to and entertaining old flames and bad boys. In obedience, I cleaned out all the old phone numbers and pictures and even blocked some because that was my clutter. That mess was blocking any possibility of God bringing my husband into my life. With the old men completely out of my life, I had made room for the man that God would eventually bring.

What: Clutter exists in every area of our lives in some way, shape, or form. Much like the realistic clutter that occurs in a room, you usually start out with a clean and organized space. Then, over time, things just start to pile up. Before you even realize it, the mess has gotten out of control and now you have to call in backup or utilize an entire day just to regain order. Do not restrict your clutter to the reality of something like a room. It could totally be that, but it could also be so much more. What is something you've been praying and asking God for? What is something you've been wanting to pursue or accomplish? Is there a place you've been wanting to go or a desire you've had in your heart? These are all questions that will lead you to discover what your clutter is that's blocking you from receiving those desires.

Where: We know that clutter will not only be limited to the physical. It is important to find out what your clutter is so that you can know where you should start with the organization process. If your clutter is too much time on social media, then you will realize that your time is cluttered. If your clutter is over - indulgence in food, then you will realize that your eating habits are cluttered. What could you do with the extra time you will have once you clean out your time clutter by reducing your social media use? How could your relationship with food and your body change once you clean out the clutter of constant overeating? Realize that clutter can come in many forms - spiritual, reality, relational, personal, time, and more. No matter where in your life you find clutter, remember that it is taking up prime space for the things God has for your life.

When: Deal with clutter consistently. Don't attack everything at once when it comes to clutter. That is a sure way to get overwhelmed very quickly. Take one thing at a time. Decide and even pray on what is the most cluttered area of your life, and then commit to working in that one area only. Then, move on to the next cluttered area only once you have completely unclut-tered the previous area. We all know what it's like to do a five-minute pick up. It works for a day or two, but eventually you have to go back to that room and deep clean it out, throw some things away, and organize that room. Therefore, do not get into the habit of finding quick fixes with the clutter in your life. Commit to getting it clean and reassessing to keep it orderly, and you will reap the benefits. I will say that these kinds of situations are great to work through with a mentor or in discipleship. Often times, it's difficult for us to see our own mess (especially when we don't want to). However, a mentor will be able to shine light on problem areas and provide accounta-bility.

Why: Making room for expectancy is a mindset change. If you've been through some difficult circumstances, you can tend to think (or the enemy makes you think) that you've have been dealt the short stick in life or that you aren't worthy to be blessed. That is so far from God's heart for you. Making room for expectancy shifts your thoughts from what you lack to what you actually have. It puts power behind your words. Teach your chil-dren how to make room for expectancy, and change the generations follow-ing you.

Let's Connect it to Scripture:

♥ Psalm 62:5 (NIV) – "Find rest, O my soul, in God alone; for my hope comes from Him."
♥ Proverbs 10:28 – "The hopes of the godly result in happiness, but the expectations of the wicked come to nothing."
♥ Romans 15:13 – "I pray that God, the source of hope, will fill you completely with joy and peace because you trust in Him. Then you will overflow with confident hope through the power of the Holy Spirit."

Let's Walk it Out:

Let's take a clutter inventory now. Think about all the different areas in your life. What do you think is your most cluttered area? Pray and ask God to reveal to you what area of your life needs attention and write His response.

_____

_____

_____

_____

_____

_____

Sign _____

Date_____

Make Room for Expectancy

Let's Write it Out:

1. What have today's scriptures revealed to you about who God is?

2. What is something that you have been wanting? How can you clear out clutter to make room for it in your life?

Let's Pray it Out:

Lord, you are so awesome and wonderful. I confess that I have carried way too much clutter in my life. Forgive me for allowing the fear of change to hold me back from making room for the good things that you have for me. I pray that you would reveal to me where the clutter is and help me to clear it out for you. My hope is in you, Lord. Thank you for desiring to give me good things. Amen.

Day Fifteen

Discover Your Gifts

Who doesn't love gifts? I personally like giving them more than receiving them. Although, there's just something about getting a gift from someone and knowing that they got that gift specifically with you in mind. I'm smiling just thinking about how good it feels when someone hands me an unexpected gift. I hope you are smiling, too, because the great thing is that our Father God has also given each of us specific gifts. This idea used to really perplex me. I was never quite sure what a gift was versus a talent or a skill. So, it was confusing for me to understand what exactly my gifts were. I've learned that a skill is something you do, while a strength is a personal characteristic that makes up who you are. For example, I am adventurous. That is one of my strengths. I bake really well; that would be a skill that I have. A talent is usually derived from genetics, family background, or training. I have a natural talent in writing. While all of these are God-given, it is the spiritual gift given by the Holy Spirit that is purposed to be used for God's work.

Later in this chapter, we will get into exactly what types of spiritual gifts the Bible shares with us. For now, I want you to start thinking about what your skills, strengths, talents, and gifts may be. It's also important to know and believe that you have all of these. God's desire is to use you and your gifts, talents, strengths, and skills. Accordingly, discovering what yummy goodness is packed inside of you is essential. I didn't discover everything all at one time. In fact, it's been over the course of my life that I have realized my gifts, talents, strengths, and skills. Therefore, do not be disappointed if you feel like your list of awesomeness is incomplete. Many times, God needs you to develop and learn how to properly use what you already have before He adds on something else.

If you've already got a pretty good list going, then how are you using them? Even more importantly, are you using them in a way that would honor God? Maybe you want to use them in an honoring way, but you aren't sure how to do that. As long as it's done with the right heart, you can never go wrong with serving someone. Take your gifts, talents, strengths and skills, and try to use them in ways that will serve, help, and encourage someone else. Not only will you be blessing so many people, but you will also be testing out a way to operate in what you have. It will come naturally to you, and it will also bring you a feeling of joy. There are several key scriptures that discuss spiritual gifts. As you study them, keep in mind that these may not be all of the gifts, but it does give us a great idea of how we are all gifted and how they must work together.

Let's Break it Down:

How: Discovering your gifts can be both fun and frustrating at the same time. I used to be baffled at how I was supposed to figure this information out. I felt like I needed some sort of complex algorithm in order to get any answers. This part is simple though. To discover your gifts, talents, skills, and strengths, take an honest inventory of yourself. Start asking yourself questions like: What am I naturally good at that perhaps runs in the family or because I trained hard? What is a skill that I can do with little effort? What is a part of my character that portrays itself in nearly everything I say or do? What is a gift that tends to show up in ministry or service to others?

Another way to discover your rock star list is to take an assessment. I've taken several over the years. Some are to identify your possible spiritual gifts, while others will explain your personality, job preference, or temperament. Another way is to connect with your mentor or someone you are close to, such as a sibling or friend. They will often see things in you that you may have a difficult time recognizing. Actually, one of the best ways to learn your gifts is to go straight to God and ask.

What: This is not about you getting the gifts that you want. It's about you discovering everything that God has already placed inside of you. You are literally oozing awesomeness. You must realize this. So don't worry about what the gift is in comparison to someone else's. Remember, comparison is a joy stealer, and it will keep you from being excited about all the good things that you do have inside of you. Discover your gifts, realize they are great, and then stay in your lane and operate in them. When you use what God has given you the way He wants you to, you are literally capable of changing the world around you.

Where: Once you discover your gifts, you can use them anywhere. Remember that God has no limits. If He gives you boundaries it is for a purpose. Follow His lead, and take into consideration that your gifts, talents, skills, and strengths may not all be used in the same place. You may use one or two in one area and another set in a completely different area of your life.

When: Take discovering your gifts seriously. Don't you want to know the gift that God thought you were special enough to hold? Aren't you curious about why you are always so energetic? Maybe you're wondering why you have a knack for negotiating. When you finally discover your gifts, you'll want to use them the way God intended. So start praying, start asking questions, start taking assessments, and prepare to be amazed by what you discover has been inside of you all along.

Why: It's a great thing to discover your gifts because the church body needs you. Each of us has a specific role to play in the church. Just like the arm is almost useless without the hand, so it is with the church body when a member does not walk in their gift. No pressure, but let's not leave the church body crippled. When we all join together, all fully functioning as one, we are much more equipped for God's work. However, if the hand is not operating correctly, the arm will suffer. Therefore, commit to discovering your gifts and being a functioning part of the church body.

Let's Connect it to Scripture:

♥ Ephesians 4:7 – "However, He has given each one of us a special gift through the generosity of Christ.""
♥ 1 Corinthians 12:7 – "A spiritual gift is given to each of us so we can help each other. To one person the Spirit gives the ability to give wise advice; to another the same Spirit a message of special knowledge. Then the same Spirit gives great faith to another, and to someone else the one Spirit gives the gift of healing. He gives one person the power to perform miracles, and another the ability to prophesy. He gives someone else the ability to discern whether a message is from the Spirit of God or from another spirit. Still another person is given the ability to speak in unknown languages, while another is given the ability to interpret what is being said. It is the one and only Spirit who distributes all these gifts. He alone decides which gift each person should have."
♥ James 1:17 – "Whatever is good and perfect is a gift coming down to us

from God our Father, who created all the lights in the Heavens. He never changes or casts a shifting shadow."

♥ Romans 11:29 – "For God's gift and His call can never be withdrawn."

Let's Walk it Out:

Now that we know how important it is to discover your gifts, let's not waste time. Stop and pray now; ask God to reveal to you what some of your gifts are. Wait and listen, and then write His response below:

_____

_____

_____

_____

_____

_____

Sign _____

Date_____

Let's Write it Out:

1. What have today's scriptures revealed to you about who God is?

2. What is a strength, skill, talent, or gift that you have realized that you have? How can you use this and honor God? Pray about it.

Let's Pray it Out:

God, you are so kind and generous. Please forgive me for being a bad steward of the gifts that you have graciously given me. I pray that you would reveal to me what my gifts are and give me the courage to walk them out in my life in service to you and others. Thank you for your grace that is always giving me what I don't deserve. Let my life be a gift to you. Amen.

Day Sixteen

Get in Community

"No man is an island, we can be found. No man is an island, let your guard down. You don't have to fight me, I am for you. We're not meant to live this life alone." That is a line from the song "No Man is an Island" by Tenth Avenue North. It resonates with how a lot of us feel at times. We often feel alone and afraid with our guards up, not willing to let anyone get close to us. In fact, that was me for many years. I had been hurt repeatedly by my church family over the years, and it was something that made me want to retreat from attempting to build actual real relationships. Sure, I would go to church every Sunday and maybe say hello to a few people afterwards. Then, I would bolt to my car and off to my isolated world. It's a scary place to feel alone in the world - afraid to trust anyone with your thoughts, your secrets, and your fears. I lived that life for a very long time. What I learned is that by guarding myself from experiencing pain again, I was also guarding myself from experiencing joy and happiness.

That song says it crystal clear – "We're not meant to live this life alone." We were creatively designed to live this life in fellowship and relationship with each other. In fact, it is actually scientifically proven that human beings need relationships with other people. There are even animals that operate this same way. Dolphins travel in pods in order to feed, breed, and provide protection. This is much like us; we need people to help us survive. Of course, it is possible to live an isolated life alone, but it surely would not be a thriving, healthy life. For humans, relationships also provide food (spiritual, physical, mental, emotional), breeding opportunities, and some forms of protection. Not only are we designed for relationship with each other, but we are primarily designed for relationship with God. This desire is at the very core of our being, and our relationship with Him helps form how we handle relationships with others. Hence, if your relationship with God is a little off in some way, it will affect your relationships with others.

This is why it's such a good thing to get into the community. When I talk about community here, I am primarily referring to your church community and the importance of getting involved in church outside of Sunday attendance. However, I am not discrediting the need for other types of community involvement. Just remember that your church family is your family, and developing those relationships should be a priority. If you've been hurt by your church family, I can relate. It's almost like being hurt by a blood relative. Understand that your church family is human; they are sinners just like you. Therefore, offenses and wrongdoings will always occur. Please be quick to address it, if necessary, forgive, and move on with your life.

In some cases, it helps to stop being so easily offended. The enemy loves to cause division, especially among believers. He knows that we are much more powerful and effective for the Kingdom when we work together. Alone, we are vulnerable to attack and too weak to fight. Remember, if you have any fear about getting into the community, it is a strategic move by the enemy to paralyze you from moving forward. Because we are designed for community involvement, there are some things that God will only bring forth in your life through community. Still, the devil will tamper with those plans. After I had a couple of bad experiences at church, I went into isolation from my church family. For a year or two, I felt God convicting me to get back active, but I was full of fear and a little bitter. Because of this, I was hesitant, and I kept putting it off by telling myself that they didn't need me. Since you can never really reject God, He eventually found a way to get me into community. I was a little nervous about it, but I saw the need and knew that I was helping fill it. Subsequently, it became more about serving others and less about me.

That one step into community opened the door to so many blessings in my life - many of which I am still experiencing today. Words and prophecies were spoken over me. I never would have gotten them had I not been in community, friendships, and relationships with amazing people. It even helped me grow spiritually and socially. I am now in the pack. I look back at my old, isolated self, and I feel sad for her. She was alone and felt invisible. Oh, but the devil is a lie! Today, I'm in community, and I'm thriving like never before. Believe me - if I can do it, I know you can, too.

Let's Break it Down:

How: Getting into community is easy. The hard part is breaking the mindsets that have kept you out of community. I've had friends say they will get into community when they lose weight or when they have more time. The truth is that anyone can come up with an excuse. Instead, you should make time for community even if you have to start small. Most churches have ministries that run through the work of volunteers. Find one that you would enjoy, and then sign up. Let me warn you that it will probably make you uncomfortable on some level, but remember that growth happens outside of your comfort zone. So let's get uncomfortable! Another way to jump into community is through a life group or Bible study. Usually these are grouped by age, sex, marital status, or even by hobbies. Either way, find one that you want to try out, and then go for it. These are not jobs; so you don't have to commit to the first one you try out. Keeping checking out different ones until you find one that you enjoy.

What: Community is several things. First, it's a place that you can connect with other believers and actually form friendships. Church on Sunday is usually a hustle and bustle, and it may be difficult trying to connect with people when everyone is going and coming. Community is also a place where you can worship with other believers. Yes, you do that on Sundays, but you do not want to be a "Sunday Christian." Connecting with other believers in community during the week provides refreshment and encouragement between Sunday gatherings. Community also is a place where God moves and where growth can happen. Just like any Father, God loves when His children get together. Often times, He will give your church family a word of encouragement or something meaningful and personal to share with you. This is a place where you can share troubles and struggles with each other and pray for each other. It's also where you can discuss Biblical topics and get questions answered.

Where: Community happens everywhere. Depending on how you choose to jump into community, you may find yourself at someone's house or at a park. You may even end up staying at church an extra hour or two or sitting in a local taco shop. It does not matter where community happens; it just matters that it does happen. I've actually found that it makes being in community even more fun when the meet up place is changed from time to time.

When: Usually life groups and Bible studies are on a set schedule. It's best to be consistent once you find one that you like. Because this is our church family, be vocal about when you may not be able to make it. Once they get used to seeing you, they will expect you to show up, and they will become concerned if they do not hear from you. For other ministries or serving opportunities, there is usually a sign up that allows you to choose how frequently you serve. This is often changeable. So choose what feels comfortable for you starting out, and then make changes if needed.

Why: Please don't miss the importance of this topic. Seek community sooner rather than later. You have no idea the blessings and growth that will come out of it. Yes, it means exposing yourself to the possibility of getting hurt, but it also means exposing your heart to the definite chance that you will be blessed. Remember, we were not designed to live life alone. You may meet your future husband or a mentor in community. God may be ready to provide you with the very thing that you need right now through community. Take the step of faith, and trust God that it will be for your good and His glory.

Let's Connect it to Scripture:

♥ Hebrews 10:24-25 – "Let us think of ways to motivate one another to acts of love and good works. And let us not neglect our meeting together, as some people do, but encourage one another, especially now that the day of His return is drawing near."
♥ Romans 12:16 – "Live in harmony with each other. Don't be too proud to enjoy the company of ordinary people. And don't think you know it all!"
♥ Acts 2:46 - "They worshipped together at the Temple each day, met in homes for the Lord's Supper, and shared their meals with great joy and generosity."
♥ James 5:16 – "Confess your sins to each other and pray for each other so that you may be healed. The earnest prayer of a righteous person has great power and produces wonderful results."

Get In Community

Let's Walk it Out:

It's time to get excited about community! Take some time to meditate and pray over what your first step into community will be. Write your thoughts and God's response below:

_____

_____

_____

_____

_____

_____

Sign _____

Date_____

Let's Write it Out:

1. What have today's scriptures revealed to you about who God is?

2. What has been your biggest fear about jumping into community? Pray and ask God to replace that fear with His peace.

Let's Pray it Out:

Heavenly Father, you are so awesome and amazing. Forgive me for turning my back on community. Thank you for designing the church family to operate as one and be an extension of family. Please highlight a place where I can get into community and grow. Amen.

Day Seventeen

Guard Your Heart

In the physical sense, the heart is a very important organ to the body. It is solely responsible for pumping blood and nutrients to the rest of the body to ensure that it functions properly. This pumping happens naturally - we do not have to think about it or program it. Usually, no one even thinks about the importance of the heart until it actually begins to have a problem. On the emotional side of things, however, the heart is what everyone wants to live by. "Follow your heart!" or the "The heart wants what it wants!" have become common sayings in culture today. While it sounds good, it isn't quite God, and that is a big problem.

Unfortunately, today's focus on the heart is upside down. Instead of putting so much emotional stock into the heart, we should be investing in the heart spiritually. The Bible has a lot to say about the heart. I'm sure most of you have even heard the very common and Biblically based statement, "Guard your heart." Just as it is a key organ of our physical bodies, it is also a key organ for our spiritual being. This is a reason why the breastplate of righteousness is so important in our armor. It's time to get diligent about guarding our hearts. This is a task that only you can accomplish. Much like giving birth, only you can protect your heart. Your mom can't do it for you, your pastor can't do it for you, and God won't do it for you. Why? Because He has already given you every tool necessary for you to be able to guard your own heart. This is the same heart that He entrusted to you, the same heart that He enables to beat to a perfect rhythm. In the same way that you must be a good steward of the body that God gave you, you must also be a good steward of the heart that He gave you, spiritually and physically.

Guarding your heart occurs on several different playing fields. For a time, I struggled with this in my dating relationships. I'll first admit that none of these men were right for me, but I went against God's will full speed ahead (I do not recommend that ever). My issue was that I would quickly give my heart away to these men. They put forth little effort and had not even proven themselves to be worthy recipients, and yet I would throw my whole heart at them and later wonder why I was a broken mess. It took me some time to uncover the deeper importance of this lesson. What I eventually learned (after repeated mistakes) was that my lack of caution in guarding my heart stemmed from the fact that I did not feel very valuable. My heart attitude about myself was that I didn't have much worth. So, when it came to relationships, I was careless with my heart because I didn't think it was worth protecting. I felt like I had to prove to these men that I was worthy of their attention. I did that by giving them access to something that they did not deserve and did not know how to treasure: my heart.

Had I been more aware of the consequences of not guarding my heart, I would have saved myself a lot of pain. The first thing is that I needed to know and believe my worth and value. Once I did this, it would utterly change everything about my relationships with men. I found my worth and value as I spent time with Jesus in His Word. I realized how special I was to Him and how much He loved me. His love replaced the thought that I had no worth. Once this shift occurred, I no longer gravitated towards relationships with those types of men at all. In fact, I could spot a counterfeit seducer easily. I no longer fell victim to the silly lines and bad boy image. I knew that I was a precious jewel in the eyes of Jesus, worthy only of a prince crafted by Him. I no longer had the desire to waste my royalty on men that were not on my level. Guarding your heart is essential, and it's important that you immediately begin doing so.

Let's Break it Down:

How: Guarding your heart requires deliberate action. Whatever flows from the heart affects your whole being. So, it's important to survey what you are feeding to your heart and how you are conditioning it. Porn, vulgar music, and toxic relationships all have the ability to feed your heart. Once something takes root in your heart, it controls and affects every aspect of your life. Cursing becomes normal, and you stop even noticing when people curse because your heart has been conditioned for it. That toxic relationship begins to feel normal, because you have conditioned your heart to accept mistreatment. Therefore, it is important to condition your heart God's way in order to shield it from the gunk that floats around in our world today. Much like cardio conditions the heart to physically function well, our hearts also require spiritual conditioning. To condition your heart, you must flood it daily with the Word of God. The power of God's Word will wash away the grime of the world and give your heart a new makeover. It will cause you to desire the things that God desires and to dislike the things that God dislikes. When your heart is spiritually conditioned, it will be strong and able to withstand against the dark influences of the world.

What: There are many areas that will require your attention when guarding your heart. It is your heart that stores forgiveness, bitterness, anger, hate, and many other emotions triggered by your thoughts. You cannot necessarily stop people from hurting you or prevent yourself from experiencing painful things. However, you can control your heart's response to them. It takes a lot of practice to not hold onto bitterness, anger, and other emotions when you feel them. Nevertheless, when your heart is conditioned, you will have more strength to feel the emotions without allowing them to settle in your heart and cause damage.

Where: The heart operates alone. If it stops beating, it is only a mere few minutes before the body begins to die. In the event of an emergency, resuscitation can occur. However, this happens only by physically or electrically creating a pump well enough that it produces the strength to get blood and nutrients to the body as normal. It is a sick heart that stops beating. Sometimes the problem is very straightforward and obvious, and other times it's hidden and requires some research to discover the issue before it causes a major problem. Sometimes a sickness will be one thing but manifest itself in a completely different way. So it is with the spiritual heart. What's at the core of your heart issue may be difficult to see because it's manifesting itself in a different way. This was the case with my heart issue in relationships. I determined that my heart was sick because I did not feel valued. Later, I dug deeper and uncovered that my real heart issue stemmed from a resentment I had against my dad. Just like an AED shock or a CPR chest compression, the Holy Spirit is always ready to help you get your heart back in the proper operating condition.

When: Heart conditions are a serious concern in the physical realm and should be just as serious in the spiritual realm. Just as a heart disease diagnosis would prompt a doctor to prescribe medications and a heart healthy diet, a spiritual heart disease diagnosis should also prompt you to respond accordingly. People who are diagnosed with heart disease typically do not sit around and wait for something drastic to happen before they take action. Hence, when you discover that you haven't been guarding your heart so well, do not wait to change and risk the damage of a sick heart. Start immediately working on guarding your heart.

Why: The heart affects the way you function physically and spiritually. If you haven't been physically conditioning your heart, you will be easily winded when you exert energy. Likewise, if you haven't been guarding your heart spiritually, you will be easily moved by your thoughts and emotions. Do not trust your heart as a definitive authority on anything. Invest your heart in God and His Word, and let Him guide you in the way you should feel, the things you should say, and the way you should act.

Let's Connect it to Scripture:

♥ Proverbs 3:5 – "Trust in the Lord with all your heart; do not depend on your own understanding."
♥ Proverbs 4:23 – "Guard your heart above all else, for it determines the course of your life."
♥ Romans 12:2 – "Don't copy the behavior and customs of this world, but let God transform you into a new person by changing the way you think. Then you will learn to know God's will for you, which is good and pleasing and perfect."
♥ Psalm 51:10 – "Create in me a clean heart, O God. Renew a loyal spirit within me."

Let's Walk it Out:

It's time to get your guard up, because your heart needs protecting. Have you been complacent in guarding your heart? What damage has your heart suffered? Are you ready to invest your heart in God and let Him fix your heart issue? Take some time in prayer to allow God to show you the weak areas of your heart. Write His response below.

_____

_____

_____

_____

_____

_____

Sign _____

Date_____

Let's Write it Out:

1. What have today's scriptures revealed to you about who God is?

2. What step do you need to take to fix your heart issue and begin conditioning your heart?

3. What is one area of your life that has affected by your heart issue? How will conditioning your heart create growth and change in this area?

Let's Pray it Out:

Father, you are my Wonderful Counselor and Savior. Forgive me for not taking care of my heart. Thank you for not only being my friend, but also the healer and lover of my soul. Help me by the power of your Holy Spirit to guard my heart as I invest it more and more into You and Your Word. You are worthy of all the praise and honor.

Day Eighteen

Live with Purpose (Intent)

This may sound silly, but since there is no such thing as a stupid question, bear with me for a moment. Did you know that the word *purpose* is both a noun and a verb? I'll admit that for years the word *purpose* existed only as a verb in my vocabulary. I know a few of you must relate, right? Well, when I realized that it was also a noun, I was shell-shocked. I've learned that the noun version is defined as "the reason for which something is done or created or for which something exists." The verb version is defined as "one's intention or objective." Now, I actually cannot take full credit for this discovery. This revelation was actually revealed to me at a purity conference that I attended at the young age of thirty-two. It was honestly like a paradigm shift for me; it literally caused a shift in the way that I lived my life and the action of positioning my will over my emotions and feelings. Consequently, the statement "purpose in your heart" has stuck with me ever since.

This was especially important for someone like me since my emotions can often get the best of me. It was a game-changer to understand that I could actually override my obnoxious emotions and get things accomplished. Understand that this isn't just about getting things accomplished. It's actually much bigger than that. It's about your life. I want to share with you a conversation that I recently had with my daughter. It went a little something like this:

Do you know that your life does not just happen? Your life is not a movie that has been carefully scripted, nor is it a jumble of random happenings. There is a time in everyone's life when they become able to make their own decisions. It's a time that comes before voting age or even driving age. It is that age when you are coherently able to truly decipher between right and wrong and make your own choices. Typically, this age is around middle school when puberty is settling. This is the stage when we all discover ourselves outside of our parent's identity. It's when we begin thinking about

111

who we are, who we want to be, and who we will turn out to be. It's a moment of self-discovery, newfound freedom, and expression. It's the moment when purpose separates into a noun and a verb whether we are ready for it or not.

It's key at this point that you realize that we all have a purpose on this Earth. It goes beyond being a doctor or vacationing in the Caribbean. It's so much bigger that. But, how do you get there? Especially if you are not even sure where you are going? You must realize that your life is formed out of the decisions and the choices you make. To tell a lie, to go to that bar, to blow that money all adds up and leads you to a certain destination. I believe this is at the core of the "mid-life crisis" for many. People go through the motions of living their lives haphazardly, and then they wake up one day and realize that their lives are nothing like they thought they would be. Then, comes the downward spiral, the disruption of the family, and the emotional turmoil that can last for quite some time and leave a trail of damage in the aftermath.

This is why it's so important that you are able to differentiate between *purpose* the noun and *purpose* the verb. Then, learn how to live with purpose. Stop going through the motions and expecting things to just turn out great. You must purpose in your heart to be sure that your choices line up with God and His will for your life. This act of the will has to override your own thoughts, emotions, and desires. It's much like taking a long road trip. Once you've determined your destination, you need a route. Your GPS map provides you with the best route, and you get on the road and follow the map. Even if you experience unexpected traffic, a flat tire, or if you end up in an unfamiliar area, you still follow the map because you know it's your best bet to get to where you are going. This is living with purpose.

It's going with God's map, even if you're a little nervous about the direction. The great thing about God's map is that it's much like the GPS map. If you get off course, you can be confident that He will recalculate your route and get you back on the right road. What makes God's map so exciting is that it's never just about the destination. He actually cares about your journey to the destination just as much. So, you can be assured that in your journey, He is filling you, molding you, and preparing you so that you will be more than ready when you finally reach your destination.

Let's Break it Down:

How: To live with purpose does not mean that you turn off your emotions. God created emotions. He wants us to be able to feel warmth when we are embraced by a loved one or joy when a baby is brought into the world. It's these emotions that allow us to experience relationships with each other and with Him. However, our emotions were never created to rule our lives. This is why our will to live by God's design must be stronger than our own feelings and emotions. To live with purpose, choose to master your decisions so that they match God's desires for you, and then learn to act on them.

What: Has God told you to do something? Has He given you a vision? Even if you are not clear on the exact direction, He has always given enough information for you to take the first step. It was the Purity Conference that first ignited purpose in my heart to remain abstinent until marriage. This decision was not because I hated sex nor that I had no desire for it. It was a decision solely made because I wanted to do it God's way more than I wanted to have my own way. This decision changed the way I thought about abstinence. I was no longer worried about how I would be able to maintain my vow to God. The decision actually made me feel free; it gave me peace because it was a part of God's design for me. When your choices line up with the will of God for your life, you will always have peace. Even if there is uncertainty, you will still have peace that you are moving in the right direction.

Where: When you live with purpose according to God's design, you will always end up in a good place. I will admit that it will probably not look the way you think it should, but it will always be so much better than what you could have done all by yourself. So, go wherever He leads you, and trust Him every step of the way. Remember to always be in constant communication with Him, ask questions, and remain thankful.

When: Living with purpose is a lifelong journey - you will never stop. So, always be persistent in evaluating your choices. Remember that if you get off track, God is consistently faithful to reroute you and get you back to the place that you need to be. Be careful not to deliberately create your own road. If you get cocky and decide to walk your own way, you will eventually find yourself lost and in the wrong place. In addition, you will have lost precious time in the process. Be encouraged that even when you get sassy with God, He still loves you, and He is waiting for you to turn back to Him in repentance. Expect and accept His loving correction as He takes time to reroute you.

Why: Living with purpose is a choice that everyone has to make. A purposeful choice cannot be made for you, nor can a purposeful life be lived for you. You make the decision to follow God's design on your own. Just remember that no matter what you choose, you will be responsible for it. There will be no one to blame and no one to be angry with but yourself. So, choose God's design no matter what you feel, and rejoice that your decision will bless you, your children, and your children's children.

Let's Connect it to Scripture:

♥ Psalm 57:2 – "I cry out to God Most High, to God who fulfills His purpose for me."
♥ Isaiah 55:11 – "It is the same with my Word. I send it out, and it always produces fruit. It will accomplish all I want it to, and it will prosper everywhere I send it."
♥ John 5:30 – "I can do nothing on my own. I judge as God tells me. Therefore, my judgment is just, because I carry out the will of the one who sent me, not my own will."
♥ Jeremiah 29:11 – " 'For I know the plans I have for you,' says the Lord. 'They are plans for good and not for disaster, to give you a future and a hope."

Let's Walk it Out:

It's time to live with purpose! Think of one thing you can change in your life or mindset that will help you to live with purpose right now. Pray and ask the Holy Spirit to reveal what's in your heart.

_____

_____

_____

_____

_____

_____

Sign _____

Date _____

Live with Purpose (Intent)

Let's Write it Out:

1. What have today's scriptures revealed about who God is?

2. What's one emotion you need to take master over and submit to the will of God?

3. How have your past choices shaped where and who you are today?

Let' Pray it Out:

Lord, you are faithful, just, trustworthy, and honorable. In fact, you are all this and more. Please forgive me for choosing my will and desires over your perfect plan. Thank you for loving me enough to have good plans for me. Even when I mess up, you love me still. I pray that you would give me a heart to obey you. Reveal your heart to me so that I can see myself as you see me. Amen.

Day Nineteen

Stay on the Course

So many times in our lives, we find ourselves at a crossroad. Sometimes it becomes apparent immediately, and other times it just kind of sneaks up on you. It's good to realize that these crossroads are pivotal points in your life, and it's even better to be prepared to act when you come to your crossroads. Your actions should always readily line up with God and His Word. Your movement in this area can literally catapult you into your purpose and destiny. Now, the crossroad will not look inviting. In fact, it will typically be something difficult and outside of your comfort zone. This is because movement is always about letting go of a little bit more of you and getting more of God. This movement is what's intended to draw you closer to God and maturity in your faith. Regardless, of what the crossroad presents, be willing to go the way the Lord leads you, and then be committed to stay on the course.

No matter what oppositions rise up against you, know that God is for you and not against you. As long as you stay on the course as He has laid it before you, it is a guarantee that His provision, protection, and power will always be available to you. God cannot lie, and He always has good plans for you. So, decide to trust Him with the outcome and purpose to remain obedient. Many times, our crossroads come at the Lord's response to our prayers and our cries at night. God loves you, and He hears you. He is your Redeemer. Therefore, He wants you live in the light of His freedom and truth. He also desires for you to receive all the blessings that He wants to pour out on you. You must be willing to be led by Him. He will provide a way, but you are the one that will need to act. Remember, the enemy will always have an alternate plan for you. That's why it is important that you remain focused and ready to act when you arrive at your crossroad. You must decide who you will serve - yourself, the devil, or God - because that will determine who will be leading you on your journey. The outcome of your journey is dependent on who you choose to lead you through the crossroad decision.

Take the Israelites for example. They cried and cried out for God to deliver them out of slavery in Egypt. God heard them, and He responded, dynamically. He sent Moses and Aaron to pharaoh, and He showed out. Then, He led them to the land that He had promised their ancestors. God always keep His promises. Even though He was leading them and caring for them the entire time, the Israelites still had trouble staying on the course. See, God didn't share the details of the journey with the Israelites. He doesn't have to do that. It is the same thing with you. He doesn't have to share every single detail of His plan with you. He wants to see that you will trust Him. Since the Israelites didn't get the rescue they wanted, they complained at every turn. They were so unthankful for what God had already done for them. They were ungrateful, and this is what you need to guard against.

The Israelites griped, complained, and sinned so much that a three-day journey turned into forty long years in the wilderness. God couldn't bring them into the Promised Land even though He wanted to do it. They were so rebellious against Him, so He had to turn away from them. They were free, yet they chose to revert back to a slavery mindset and invited death over being free. They did so because things weren't going the way they wanted. Consequently, their rebellious actions forfeited their right to the Promised Land. Eventually, they all died and only their offspring were left to inherit the Promised Land. This is why it's crucial to stay on the course with God. If He put you there, He has a very good reason. You must trust Him to the very end. Do not forfeit your inheritance because of a rebellious spirit against the Lord. Remain thankful always and avoid complaining. Never reminisce or long for what God brought you out of previously. In addition, be careful not to turn a regular journey into multiple trips around the mountain.

Let's Break it Down:

How: Staying on course with God requires that you be in tune with Him and learn to hear His voice. Take time praying and seeking Him on a daily basis. Then, wait in silence for 2-3 minutes after you have prayed so that you can hear His response to you. Be sure to write everything down, and remain focused by staying in the Word. Commit Bible verses to memory that will serve as encouragement for you. It is also important to have someone to talk to regularly. It should be someone you can share your thoughts and emotions with during your journey. This person needs to be someone trustworthy who can pray for you, encourage you, and hold you accountable. Don't be overcome by the words of others. There may be people who will try to discourage you or distract you. Don't be moved by external things.

What: The course that God puts you on is the only course that matters. If you find yourself on your own course, then make corrections quickly. Test the course against God's word to see if it lines up. Also, pray about it and wait for God's response. It is crucial that you understand that the enemy will create fake courses that look very, very attractive. It will usually be something that will fit all your checkboxes except for one. That one is usually a super huge deal; however, if he can trick you into seeing it his way, then he has won. Remember: for everything in the natural realm, there is a something in the spiritual realm that mirrors it. When you find yourself at a crossroads to a new course, you always want to identify if this is a God course or something else.

Where: The types of crossroads and journeys that I am talking about are not physical in nature. There is no yellow brick road that is going to be laid out for you. This is not a family vacation; no one travels your course but you. So, while it's occurring in your natural life here on Earth, it has everything to do with the spiritual. It may be for growth, maturation, preparation, or healing. It could be for many other things as well. This is all according to God's own plan and design for how He wants your life to go.

When: Learning to stay on the course is a lifetime lesson. You will find yourself on different journeys with God throughout your entire life. Embrace each journey as an invitation to go deeper with Him, regardless of when the crossroad presents itself. Not all journeys are the same, nor are they for the same purpose. Sometimes your crossroad will lead you into a longer journey with God, while other times it's just for a short journey. This also depends on your heart in the journey, and your willingness to be obedient to whatever God is doing in your life at that very moment.

Why: Staying on the course has so many ramifications. It can be a hard lesson for some to learn because most of us have been conditioned by today's microwave culture. People do not want to work hard or feel uncomfortable. Usually, it is these exact types of things that produce the greatest reward. Resist the urge to back out or become bitter. I know you want to spread your wings and fly, but first allow God to take you to the place where He knows you will bloom.

Let's Connect it to Scripture:

♥ Psalm 119:1-8 (AMP Version): "[1] How blessed and favored by God are those whose way is blameless (those with personal integrity, the upright, the guileless), walk in the law (and you are guided by the precepts and revealed will) of the Lord. [2] Blessed and favored by God are those who keep His testimonies, And who (consistently) seek Him and long for HIm with all their heart. [3] They do no unrighteousness; they walk in HIs ways. [4] You have ordained your precepts, That we should follow them with (careful) diligence. [5] Oh, that my ways would be established to observe and keep your statutes (obediently accepting and honoring them)! [6] Then I will not be ashamed. When I look (with respect) to all your commandments (as my guide). [7] I will give thanks to You with an upright heart, When I learn (through discipline) Your righteous judgements (for my transgressions). [8] I shall keep your statutes; do not utterly abandon me (when I fail)."

Let's Walk it Out:

If you're at a crossroad right now in your life, stop, pray, and ask God to direct you in the right way. If you're in the journey already, pray and ask God to reveal His heart for you in this time. Wait and listen. Then, write down what you hear.

_____

_____

_____

_____

_____

_____

Sign _____

Date _____

Let's Write it Out:

1. What has today's scripture revealed to you about who God is?

2. What has your attitude been during the process that God has you on right now? Is there anything you need to ask God to forgive you for?

3. What are you struggling with the most when it comes to staying on the course with God?

Let's Pray it Out:

Dear Heavenly Father, you are so amazing and kind. Your love never fails me. Please forgive me for doubting you and your ways. Thank you for always being so gentle with me and for loving me enough to bless me with good things. Lord, I pray that you would continue to guide me and that you would give me the patience to stay on the course with you. Amen

Day Twenty

Trust the Process

Sometimes it's really hard to see the forest for the trees. This saying has been around for some time, but it's so relevant to what I want to share with you today. Imagine that God has orchestrated your life to be one big beautiful picture. He knows what will happen every minute of every day that you walk the earth, because He's planned it all. He knows what your gifts and talents are and how He wants them to manifest in your life. He also knows where you'll be in twenty years, thirty years, and so on. He loves you so much that He's taken all the guess work out of life. You don't have to chase the dreams your parents have for your life or live in the shadow of someone else. All you have to do is chase God, and He will reveal, in His own timing, the details that you need to know to move forward.

Sometimes, it can be really hard to function in life. It's especially difficult when we look at where we are and where we want to be, and feel like we've got way too far to go. Because we are up-close and personal in our lives, we have a tendency to focus so closely on smaller details that we get overwhelmed and forget that they all add up to a much bigger picture that we aren't able to see yet. We focus so much on the trees in our lives that we lose sight of the huge beautiful and blessed forest that makes up those trees. It's important to take a step back and trust the process - God's process.

I love desserts. I have a major sweet tooth, especially for cakes. Baking a cake requires a process – they don't just appear out of thin air. There is no magical recipe in existence that can produce a fluffy and delicious cake without first undergoing some sort of process, and there's good reason for it. Imagine your life is a cake. All cakes generally require the same basic ingredients - sugar, flour, butter, eggs, baking powder, salt, some form of liquid, and a fat. All of these ingredients work together to produce a flavorful, moist creation. The ingredients should be mixed in proper balance. Otherwise, the final outcome of the cake can become altered. When there is too much sugar, the texture becomes crumbly and does not hold its shape when cut. Alternatively, too little sugar results in a tougher texture than desired. Then, there is the delicate art of mixing. In addition, the oven temperature must be correct, and the pan must be the right size to hold everything and leave room for rise and expansion without overflowing.

Just like we must trust the step-by-step process of cake making, we must also trust God's step-by-step process of molding us and our lives into a beautiful thing. We know that if we cut corners on the process of making a cake, the outcome will be so much less than what it could have been. It is the same thing with our lives. If we try to take shortcuts outside of God's design, we're only cheating ourselves out of the great life God has for us. We must trust His process. We must allow God to add, take away, mix, and bake as He pleases. Let's take this simple cake process concept, and apply it to your life. In order to be the woman that God created you to be and to walk in your life's purpose, it's necessary for you to come into agreement with God so that He can add His own ingredients. There are things you will need to know, skills you will need to have, ways you will need to speak, and an attitude that you will need to possess. You will already have a lot of this, but the problem is that it's mixed wrong. Your cake is a mess, and this is why you need to allow God to have His way in your life.

Let Him have His way with your finances, your personality, your social life, your attitude and your body. As He begins to add His own ingredients, you will feel a change happening. His eggs will provide the moisture to your dry spirit. His oils will bring volume and texture to your uninspiring personality. His flour will bind together your gifts and talents for His glory and your good. The liquid He adds will fill you to overflowing with His love and grace. His added salt will give flavor to your speech, and His added sugar will produce a sweet, tender spirit. Trusting the process is a journey. All that mixing and all that baking will come to completion in God's allotted timeframe. However, if you are resistant to Him, if you are stubborn or unthankful, you could find that your process is extended.

Let's Break it Down:

How: Trusting the process is about surrender on all levels, emotionally, physically, spiritually, and mentally. I know it is easy to become a complainer. I'll admit that there was a time when I was a chronic complainer and did not even realize it until it was brought to my attention. Choose to have a thankful attitude towards the Lord, even when things are not going your way or the way that you think they should. If you need something, ask Him, but never come against the Lord in sin and disrespect. This process is a crucial step before you can possess the land God has for you. Take joy in the fact that He loves you enough to refine you so that you will be able to produce much fruit and prosper in the land that He has for you.

What: From the moment we accept Jesus' invitation for salvation, we all undergo a process. Because perfection here on earth is unattainable, we are never truly a finished work in Christ until we get to heaven. Therefore, the process continues throughout our entire life. As we go through the hills and valleys of life, God transforms us on many levels. Some will be major levels, others will not. No matter what the transformation is, the process is still important because each transformation builds upon itself. Remember the trees that make up the forest? The transformations you experience are all the trees that God is planting in the big forest (picture) of your life. It is not a requirement that you are able to recognize the picture or understand it. Your only requirement is to surrender to the process with a thankful attitude.

When: Because the process of life is continual, so is the *when*. There will be times in your life when you will feel like you are living the same day over and over. It is uncomfortable and somewhat irritating, and you cannot seem to figure out what you are doing wrong. You may be in the middle of your process. There will be other times when you can just feel the tempo of your life shifting. It is an uneasy feeling mixed with uncertainty. Your process for this season has just started if you are feeling this way. Other times, you may be feeling like it's time to make a move, like you are being gently pushed in a certain direction. You may be at the end of your process.

Where: Know that there will be different seasons of your life; therefore, different processes to match these seasons. Learn to develop a keen sense of what season you are in, because it will help you find your way in your process. Furthermore, it will help you determine what God is trying to do during your process. Remember to always resist the urge to fight God in your process. Trust that He knows exactly what you need and when you need it in order to navigate through the process with Him.

The cake making process is foundationally the same, but it can be slightly altered with different ingredients to make something else that is equally delicious. This is what you must understand about your process. Last time, maybe God was taking you through something simple like a basic yellow cake. However, the next process may be a German Chocolate cake and require a whole lot more ingredients. So, whatever processes the Lord has you dealing with, take heart that it will come out great, and don't expect every process to look the same. As you grow spiritually, it is natural for things to get more in-depth. Take that as a sign of maturity on your part, and embrace the fact that God desires to see you thrive.

Why: The process happens whether you are looking for it or not. It's essential to our spiritual growth that we understand that in order for God to get us where He needs us (and where we undoubtedly want to be) to be, we must go through some sort of process. He wants to see if you are faithful and if you can be trusted with the massive blessing He wants to give you. Therefore, trusting Him through the process can be your step into that blessing that you have been praying for. Do not take the process lightly. Decide now whether you will nurture and care for those trees in your forest or if you will let them die because you didn't trust that God could do what He said.

Let's Connect it to Scripture:

♥ Psalms 32:8 – "The Lord says, "I will guide you along the best pathway for your life. I will advise you and watch over you."
♥ Psalms 111:7-8 – "The works of His hands are faithful and just; all His precepts are trustworthy. They are steadfast forever and ever, done in faithfulness and uprightness."
♥ Psalm 125:1-2 – "Those who trust in the Lord are like Mount Zion, which cannot be shaken but endures forever as the mountains surround Jerusalem so the Lord surrounds His people both now and forever."
♥ Proverbs 16:9 – "We can make our plans, but the Lord determines our steps."

Let's Walk it Out:

It's time for some refinement! An important part of trusting the process is knowing the season you're in currently. It's hard to bake a cake and trust it'll come out right if you're not sure what the cake is. Pause here to pray and ask God to reveal what season you are in right now. Then, write His response below:

_____

_____

_____

_____

_____

_____

Sign _____

Date _____

Let's Write it Out:

1. What have today's scriptures revealed about who God is?

2. What has been the hardest part about trusting God's process for you?

Let's Pray it Out:

Heavenly Father, you are such a great Father. You are so kind, so loving, and quick to forgive. I would be nothing without you. Lord, forgive me for fighting your process. Forgive me for thinking that I know better than you and can do it all by myself. Thank you that even when I am stubborn, you lavish me with tender love and care. I pray that my heart's desires would align with yours. Lord, I abandon my way of thinking and doing, and I surrender to your process. Amen.

Day Twenty-One

Build Your Legacy

Building a legacy is serious business and something that you will never really learn by sitting in a classroom. It's a standard of living, in my opinion, that needs to be adopted as common knowledge. Generally, though, it seems that information like this is only passed from word of mouth within families and small circles. This is why I am excited to be able to connect with you and share something astounding. We've covered so much in the past few weeks. They have been things that will empower you to get your life on track with God and blossom you into the very thing He saw as He designed you in your mother's womb. It is often said that change begins with self. So now that you have a good handle on yourself, it's time to move the focus over to your child(ren), present and future.

Setting up a life that your children can learn from now and long after you are gone is a beautiful gift. It makes me think of the quintessential woman in Proverbs 31. I'm so impressed with her; I strive to be a woman whose children bless her and whose husband praises her. She's beautiful, not because she's perfect or because she wears fine clothes. It's because she fears the Lord and is dedicated to being a woman of virtue. Building a legacy goes beyond working your nine to five job, attending church every Sunday, and having life insurance. Don't get me wrong - those are all very good things, and I hope that you are doing those things. However, they are just the start to building a legacy.

Building a legacy is about building something that can be passed on to your children, physically, emotionally, and mentally. Your children are mini world changers. It should be your desire that they impact this world on an even greater level than you did, because you were intentional about building a legacy that they could thrive in limitlessly. This is why it is so important to deal with your mess. If you are not careful, you will end up passing along to your kids every hurt, every offense, and every disappointment that you have ever experienced. You will parent from your pain and end up instilling into them everything you disdain as you try to fix your past through them. Do not parent your children out of the pains you experienced growing up. Do not pass things like fear of failure, a poverty mindset, or low self-esteem on to your children. Learn now to speak life into them. Connect with God, and let Him help you parent your kids. He will show you who they are and what their gifts are. When He does, affirm them over your children by speaking them out to them and encouraging them.

Parenting is a sort of trial by error journey. There is no definitive parenting manual out there that is going to tell you the exact way to parent your children so that you raise perfect human beings. This type of manual doesn't exist, because there is no such thing as perfect parenting or perfect human beings. All of us sin and fall short. It is only by God's grace and the power of the Holy Spirit in us that we are not out of control. This is why you must connect with God, even in parenting. So, what's so special about this Proverbs 31 woman? The Bible says, "She is of noble character." That means that she is honorable, self-sacrificing, gracious, and highborn. She uses her time wisely and yet her hands are always busy. She is resourceful in life to the blessing of her husband and children. She isn't lazy or held down by her past, because she has risen above it. The Lord blesses everything she touches because she seeks His will for her life. She is charitable with a loving spirit, because she knows that she is well taken care of by her Father the King. She knows who she is and whose she is. It is important that you know who you are and whose you are so that you can parent from fullness and not from lack.

Let's Break it Down:

How: Building a legacy starts with you. First, break off old mindsets established from your past. If you are harboring forgiveness, it is imperative that you forgive anyone who has hurt you. Forgiveness does not require that you feel like doing it. It is simply an act of obedience. God continually forgives you. If He can forgive, you have to be willing to forgive also. Remember that harboring grudges can cause anger, resentment, and bitterness to manifest themselves in your body. Those emotions are a poison that will physically attack your body, so be diligent and do not drink it. Please forgive now. Then, go to God and find out what kind of parent He wants you to be. Commit to being obedient to Him in becoming that. If you are finding it difficult to let go of the things that have happened in your past, I would encourage you to seek wise counsel. This could be a trusted friend, mentor, or even a licensed therapist. Never be ashamed to seek help from others.

Build Your Legacy

Just be sure to seek wise, Godly, and Biblically-based help.

What: Now that you've addressed your issues with the past, it's time to start building. Find out who your children are physically, emotionally, and mentally. Then, be intentional in building them up to reinforce those attributes. When children are young, words have so much power over them. Because of this, never ever speak negatively. Even when they mess up, discipline them from a place of love and not anger. Never tell your child(ren) they are stupid or not good at anything. Whatever words you speak over your children while they are young will influence them as they get older. Create a motto for your family. Let it be something that embodies and guides your family and creates the type of legacy that will make a lasting impact even after you are no longer around.

Where: Building a legacy begins within your home. Even something as simple as teaching them to clean up can have a major effect on them later. Look at your home as a training ground for their life. Do you spend family time together at the table at least once a day? How long is TV time? What type of manners do they display at the table? How do they speak to one another? Whatever behavior you let loose within your house will be loosed into their lives as they grow up. Laziness, unkemptness, lack of social skills are all learned from the home. So, as you build your legacy take into account that everything you allow or don't allow in your home will be the foundation from which they grow and experience the world.

When: Your children are never too young for you to begin building a legacy for them, in fact, the younger the better. Those with teenagers can attest to the fact that kids are not so impressionable within the home after a certain age. So, count it a blessing if your kids are still at a moldable age and use this time to really build and pour into them. This is a perfect time to build into them how to honor you and respect others especially older adults. This is the path that will lead to your children calling you blessed and don't we all want that.

Why: Building a legacy has vast ramifications. God entrusted you with your children, and you will be held accountable for your dealings with them. Decide today to be intentional with them. Do not leave anything to chance. Remember that all the enemy needs is for you to slip up and leave a door cracked for him to enter through. Try to save your children from having to repeat your past mistakes or relive your past life by dedicating yourself to parenting them God's way. Set your child up to live a long life and be blessed.

Let's Connect it to Scripture:

♥ Proverbs 22:6 – "Direct your children onto the right path, and when they are older, they will not leave it."
♥ Ephesians 6:2-4 – "Honor your father and mother. This is the first commandment with a promise. If you honor your father and mother, things will go well for you, and you will have a long life here on the earth."
♥ Proverbs 29:17 – "Discipline your children, and they will give you peace of mind and will make your heart glad."
♥ Proverbs 31:26-28 – "When she speaks, her words are wise, and she gives instructions with kindness. She carefully watches everything in her household and suffers nothing from laziness. Her children stand and bless her, her husband praises her."

Let's Walk it Out:

What legacy (physical, emotional, mental) do you want to leave for your children? Pray and ask God. What steps can you take today to start building that legacy? Write your response below.

_____

_____

_____

_____

_____

_____

Sign _____

Date _____

Build Your Legacy

Let's Write it Out:

1. What have today's scriptures revealed to you about who God is?

2. When you are gone, what do you want your kids to remember about you and tell others?

3. What legacy did your parents leave you (good or bad), and how has it affected how you parent your own children?

Let's Pray it Out:

Mighty Father, wonderful in all your ways, You are King of kings and Lord of lords. You are worthy of all praise. Lord, forgive me for parenting my children from my own pain. Lord, right now I release the pain that I've been holding, and I give it to you. Please heal me from the inside. Thank you that your love is enough, and your power is enough. Through you, I can do any-thing. Because you first forgave give me, I have the strength to forgive those who have hurt me. I ask that you would reveal to me the way in which you would like me to parent my child(ren). I pray that all the ways that I deal with my child(ren) will be honoring and pleasing to you. Amen.

Day Twenty-Two

Protect Your Seed

Now that you are equipped to build your legacy, it's time to get prepared to protect it. I'll admit that the joy of parenthood can become overwhelming at times, and there may be moments when you're just trying to keep your head above the water. They call it "sink or swim" and "fight or flight" mode. It happens when your back is up against a wall and you have to create your own way out. This is usually when even the quietest of new moms finds her strength and voice; it is the rise of the mama bear. I remember the first time I found my inner mama bear. It was not pretty, and I can't pretend to be proud of it. Just the mere perception that my daughter was being threatened created a rise in me unlike anything I'd experienced before. Sure, I had been mad, even downright furious at things before in the past, but this was not the same. I became strong, fearless, and bold. No one could tell me anything; I was unstoppable with a concentrated anger. No one was going to threaten her, let alone bring her harm. Now, this sounds crazy, but there is a mama bear within every mother. It just takes longer to awaken in some.

Putting everything into perspective, try to remember that even when you transform into mama bear, you really aren't all powerful and unstoppable. The reality is that only Jesus can really provide the all-knowing, all-seeing, unstoppable power and protection that your child(ren) need. There may be times when He will give you an extra dose of strength to be the mama bear that's needed in a particular moment, but don't ever forget that you are only human and always in need of our Savior. Still, as a mother, you have a definitive role to play in protecting your child(ren). Think of your child(ren) as precious, delicate seeds. I have read tons of books on how to garden. It is actually a dream of mine to one day own a house that has everything I need to create a plentiful garden to feed my family.

After reading, I discovered that there are actually some things that grow better when planted together. Soil plays a big part in how well your garden grows. Light, water and spacing will also play a part in the success of your garden. When it comes to gardening it can get tricky. There will be times when it seems you've done everything right, and still your garden doesn't flourish. There will be other times when you go against the norm and it works out great for you. However, typically when it comes to gardening, there are some foundational principles that have been established by successful gardeners before you. They share these tips in hopes that you won't experience some of the same issues that they did. This is the same when protecting your children; you should treat them as precious seeds. Don't be afraid to take the advice of seasoned parents. Ensure they get enough light and water, and give them enough space to grow without getting choked out by weeds. Pay attention to the soil you place them in, and keep the soil fed. Sow into them generously and with love so that you will see the beautiful fruits of your labor and be joyful when harvest time has come.

Let's Break it Down:

How: Protecting your seed is not just about making sure that no one hurts them physically. It's also about being watchful over everything in your house. Pay attention to what they are watching on TV, and what music they are listening to each day. If you haven't been to church in a while, start going with your children. I haven't met one young child that does not like church. Pray with your kids. Play praise and worship music or even contemporary Christian music in your house. You have the power to set the atmosphere in your own home. Create an atmosphere that welcomes the Holy Spirit to dwell in your house with your family. Read the Bible with your children; make it a fun family activity that they look forward to every day. Show them that being a believer is not boring. This is the way to protect your seed during the delicate growing stages where the outside elements can have a negative effect on their growth.

What: In essence, you are not protecting what is seen. It is not the physical body that I am highlighting right now. You are protecting them spiritually. You are watch-guarding over their spiritual growth. As little world changers, they possess a strong untapped power that God will unleash when He is ready. Until then, be the mama bear that keeps your young daughter from being influenced by the world's definition of beautiful. Be the mama bear that watches over your son and rebukes anything that would get him to turn away from the man of God that he is growing to be.

Protect Your Seed

Where: As I mentioned before, protecting your seed should start in the home. Your home should be a sanctuary from the outside world, a place that your children find rest and nourishment (physically and spiritually). The world is an unpredictable place. So, once your children walk out of your doors, you have little to no control over their surroundings and what they may come in contact with outside of the home. This is why it's always good to pray over them, and then leave the uncontrollable things to Jesus who knows all and has the ability to always protect them.

When: If you are not already protecting the spiritual seeds of your children, start now. As children grow into pre-teens and teens, they become a little more resistant to parenting. Still, remember that there is no human that can outrun or outsmart God. Do not let a headstrong child discourage you from doing what you know you are called to do. Pray aloud and with them, and play music and have discussions that speak the Word of God into their hearts. They may not want to hear it. However, with God's guidance and because you were diligent in sowing into them, that seed will bust out and bring forth fruit no matter how bad it looks. Do what you can, and have faith in what God can do with everything else.

Why: Protecting your seed is important to your child's life – both earthly and eternally. When you are old, you will want to look back and see that all the sweat, blood, and tears that you shed to protect them spiritually has been honored by God. You will want to know that when you are gone and on your way to Heaven, that you will be able to look forward to seeing your children again when they join you there. This is why you cannot falter in protecting your seed.

Let's Connect it to Scripture:

♥ Psalm 127:3 – "Children are a gift from the Lord; they are a reward from Him."
♥ 1 Corinthians 15:33 – "Don't be fooled by those who say such things, for bad company corrupts good character."
♥ Proverbs 13:20 – "Walk with the wise and become wise; associate with fools and get in trouble."
♥ Deuteronomy 6:5-7 – "[6] And you must love the Lord your God with all your heart, all your soul and all your strength. [7] And you must commit your-selves wholeheartedly to these commands that I am giving you today. Re-peat them again and again to your children. Talk about them when you are

at home and when you are on the road, when you are going to bed and when you are getting up."

Let's Walk it Out:

Okay, mama bear, it's time to get ferocious. Think about your children and the path they are traveling. What atmosphere have you created for them? Pray about how you can change the atmosphere of your home into one that provides rest and nourishment for your children spiritually and physically. Write the response below:

_____

_____

_____

_____

_____

_____

Sign _____

Date _____

Let's Write it Out:

1. What have today's scriptures revealed to you about who God is?

2. What are some difficult topics you need to discuss with your children but have been avoiding and why?

3. Do a quick mental inventory of the things that are watched, listened to and talked about in your home. Are they spiritually nourishing your child(ren) or choking them? Decide today how you will replace the old soil, light, and water for something new and honoring to God. Write it below.

Let's Pray it Out:

Heavenly Father, you are wonderful in all your ways, amazing in love, always trustworthy, and forever my closest friend. Lord, please forgive me for not taking my parenting duties more seriously. Show me how to protect the children you gave me and to sow into their lives in a way that honors you. Reveal to me the things going on in my home that need to change, and guide me as I seek to create a restful and nourishing atmosphere. Thank you that I never need to worry or feel lost, because you are always there to guide me. Amen.

Day Twenty-Three

Get God-fidence

As daughters of the Most High God, we are something serious. When we allow the Holy Spirit to work in and through us, we are an unstoppable force that can influence everything around us. Coupled with the Holy Spirit, you are an unstoppable, unquenchable, undeniable force. That is why the enemy is usually relentless when it comes to attacking our confidence and making it a heavy topic for most women to embrace. Now, we also have to be aware that there is a confidence that this world will say is good, but it is not of God. The world likes self-confidence and tells us to believe in ourselves and our abilities. However, self-confidence is a weary place to be because it puts everything on the shoulders of a human being. Yes, human beings... You know those creations that are frail, weak, and faulty.

As we discussed in earlier days, we were never designed to walk through life alone, doing our own thing, and satisfying our own desires. Instead, we were created to live life with others and to walk intimately with our Lord. At the foundation of His plan for your life (and mine), you will find that He intends for us to walk with Him, not in front of Him and not ten miles behind Him. If this is the case, then it should stand to say that the totality of our being should also walk with Him. In addition, we do not just give God our hearts. We must also strive to surrender our bodies and minds. Therefore, the world's idea of self-confidence draws us away from the very power that comes from being connected intimately to Jesus. It is not self-confidence that helps us tackle difficulties or rise up to do great things. Realize now that anything that you have ever been able to do is in direct reflection of God's power and grace in your life. That is why it is important to always avoid the lie of self-confidence and cling boldly to God-fidence.

I personally struggled with confidence and low self-esteem for roughly fifteen years of my life. I had absolutely no idea who I was, and I had no confidence in my abilities. These feelings about myself affected every area of my life. As a result, I was unable to foster healthy relationships, and I actually gravitated towards relationships that were very toxic. I became handicapped when it came to being able to have conversations with others. Therefore, I avoided long talks with others. I also avoided making friends because I believed that I had a bad personality. I spent time looking around at other women trying to figure out how they had mastered confidence. I even tried to mimic and imitate them in speech, dress, and attitude.

It wasn't until I started drawing closer to God and having personal encounters with Him that I started to understand why confidence had failed me. Drawing on my own strength was always going to lead me down a dark path. The only way that I was able to move past this was to discover my identity in Christ. This was not an overnight journey. I was a confused and twisted person after years of trying to be confident the world's way. God had to work on every part of me, piece by piece, in order to restore and renew me to the woman that He already knew I would be because of Him. This was a slow, peaceful walk with God, and it still is today. God-fidence will open doors that no man can shut, but you first have to be willing to walk away from world's way of thinking and being.

Let's Break it Down:

How: God-fidence starts by connecting intimately with God. Connect with the fact that He already knows who you are because He created you. That laugh you hate or that ear that is bigger than the other, was created for a purpose. So, find out who God says you are. Find out how He feels about you and what He thinks about you. A lot of us did not receive the proper love and acceptance from our earthly fathers. Because of this it's difficult to understand the Father's love. I promise that it runs so deep and wide that it is unmeasurable. Lose yourself and who the world says you are, and then go to God and receive your true identity. When He gives it to you, truly receive it. Do not laugh it off; instead, embrace it, accept it, and start walking in it. You will experience an immense amount of freedom when you discover yourself in Christ. Live in that identity constantly, and seek God first for everything you do. Know that none of it would be possible if you didn't have Him.

What: Never be envious of the world and its ways. You will see tons of people doing it the world's way. They will be seemingly succeeding, but know that their end will not be a glorious one. We were all created to walk with

God. Celebrities, millionaires, politicians, and regular people are all the same in the eyes of God. He loves us all the same and desires us all to be in relationship with Him. It may look like the celebrities, the millionaires, and the politicians have it all, but if they are not walking with God, they have nothing and are really missing out. Succeeding to the world and succeeding to God are very different. Never be concerned or envious of the world and its possessions. With God-fidence, you can be assured that God will do great things in and through you.

Where: God-fidence is a total body makeover. It requires you to read your Word regularly and spend time with God. Remember, when you get saved, it's not just about the heart. This is the time to be conscious of all the areas of your life. Be intentional in surrendering them to the love of Jesus. It is there that you will find your God-fidence.

When: The great thing about God-fidence is that it is yours when it finally grabs a hold of you. You will realize that no one can take away what has been redeemed to you through your confidence in God's ability. The world's confidence comes with labels and stereotypes; God-fidence is all about grace. You will not have to struggle with comparison and inadequacy once your God-fidence has been established. You will always find peace and joy in the growth you experience when you are tapped into it. You will have no more time to worry about what someone else is doing or how you will impress people and get them to like you. God-fidence says that you can do anything through Christ because He strengthens you. Additionally, there comes a great freedom in living to please God and not man.

Why: Accessing your God-fidence is about expressing your freedom. In a world where false identities are continually forced onto us, it is important to know who you are, and then boldly live it out. That is God-fidence, and it is transferrable. Your children will see you live out God-fidence, and they will know that it is a good thing. Your God-fidence can touch the lives of others around you simply by the way you are living your life. So many people today are living in bondage, trapped within themselves. They need to see Jesus in you. What better way than to live boldly as the person He designed you to be.

Let's Connect it to Scripture:

♥ John 8:36 – "So if the Son sets you free, you are truly free."
♥ Philippians 4:13 – "For I can do everything through Christ, who gives me strength."
♥ 2 Corinthians 12:9 – "Each time He said, 'My grace is all you need. My power works best in weakness.' So now I am glad to boast about my weaknesses, so that the power of Christ can work through me."
♥ Luke 1:38 – "Mary responded, 'I am the Lord's servant. May everything you have said about me come true.' And then the angel left her."

Let's Walk it Out:

It's time to get God-fidence! Right now, I want you to stop and pray. Take some time and adore the Lord, and then ask Him who you are. Get specific with your questions, because He wants to tell you the answers. He wants you to know who you are in Him. Write His response below.

_____

_____

_____

_____

_____

_____

Sign_____

Date_____

Let's Write it Out:

1. What have today's scriptures revealed to you about who the Lord is?

2. How has believing in the world's confidence kept you from being free to be who you are?

3. What area of your life have you not surrendered to the love of Christ?

Let's Pray it Out:

Heavenly Father, you are wonderful in all your ways and worthy of the highest praise. Lord, forgive me for falling captive to the world's lies and allowing them to control me. Right now, Lord, I surrender my heart, my mind, and my body to your loving provision and redemption. I want to be free to be the woman you made me to be. Lord, speak identity over me and realign my heart with yours that I may walk boldly and intimately with you now and forever. Amen.

Day Twenty-Four

Get Personal with Your Best Friend

As women, we just love to talk. It usually doesn't matter how or where you grew up. It's just a part of our make up as emotional beings to want to talk to someone. It's a beautiful thing when we can learn to channel it in a Godly way. I was a very timid child, and even though I was fearful to talk to most people, there was always at least one person in my life that I could gab away with about anything. I could call this person my best friend. I often wonder how the term *best friend* came to be. It seems that it's programmed into little girls the moment they enter the playground. We automatically have this desire to have a best friend. Often times, before we even hit the playground and are still shuffling around at home, we even create this best friend. You know what I'm talking about; the imaginary friend that played dolls with you or the doll that you sat with and talked to while you ate lunch. From a very small little girl we all develop this desire to have a best friend.

It's true that all women (and even men) need supportive, like-minded women to walk in friendship with consistently. Women need the community of other women. Whether your circle is big or small, I'm sure you have at least one woman that you know you can talk to personally. This is an important part of community as a whole. It's good to realize that not every woman you encounter will be someone with whom you will get personal. The Lord is always working and has different reasons that He allows people to cross paths with you. As young teenage girls, we have gotten the idea that everyone must like us and that we have to be friends with everyone. The truth is that it is impossible and even dangerous to be friends with everybody. Of course, it's important to be kind, peaceful, and loving towards all, friends or foes, but also learn to discern the type of relationship that God wants you to have with each other. Beyond that, embrace the truth that Jesus is your first best friend, and He is the most important best friend.

Think about your earthly best friend, how cool she is, how easy it is to talk to her, and what a pleasure it is to be around her. Now, think of Jesus and know that He is all of that and then some. Everything you talk to your earthly best friend about, you can also discuss with Jesus. There is no need to get hung up over wordy, religious prayers. This is an important part of your walk. Learn to get comfortable with getting personal with Him. Often times, people come under the misconception that Jesus only cares about you when you're misbehaving or doing something really good. This is so not true. He actually cares about you and everything about you, much like your best friend but better.

I remember one occasion when I went to a purity conference with a singles group, and God spoke to me mightily. It changed a piece of my heart. That day, He didn't only speak to me about my purity or desire to get married. He also spoke to me about my diet. It was incredibly intriguing because I was struggling with food at the time. Going to that conference, I was excited to meet with God, and I knew He would speak to my heart. However, I wasn't expecting Him to bring up something about my diet. This is how much God cares for us. He used the conference because it was a moment where my heart was actually positioned to listen to Him.

In that moment, I realized that God wanted to live life with me. If He cared so much about me that He would address my issues with food and tell me how to make changes, then surely there was so much more about my life that He wanted to discuss with me. It was then that I had a desire to get personal with Jesus. I wanted to make Him my best friend. What does it mean, what does it even look like when you make Jesus your best friend? Well, you imagine He's a friend who knows everything, and He is everywhere you go. Then, you begin to share your most inner thoughts, fears, and desires with Him. He already knows all of this, but it warms His heart when you reach out to Him. Remember, He is a gentleman and will never push Himself onto you. Yet, He is always waiting eagerly, hoping you'll receive His invitation for friendship.

Let's Break it Down:

How: Getting personal with Jesus as your best friend isn't made up of religious prayers. It's simply opening up to Him and talking with Him the way you would talk to your own earthly best friend. Sit down and have coffee or tea with Him. Sometimes people feel like they cannot talk to God about everything, but this is not true. Just like you would tell your best friend when you are struggling with lust or spent too much money on a purse, God wants you to talk with Him like this. What makes it even better is that this friendship is with the Almighty, not some imperfect human who is bound to hurt you or give you bad advice, even if it's on accident. A friendship with God opens up the realm of divine communication. This type of communication is not available here on earth. It has power, and you become privy to that power when you allow Jesus to become your best friend.

What: Friendship means a lot of different things to different people. There are people who go through their whole lives and never experience the closeness of real authentic friendship. There are others who have many friends but are afraid to truly open up to anyone. You have to determine if your idea of friendship may be tainted by bad experiences or the lack of experience at all. Your idea of what it means to get personal with an earthy best friend could hinder your ability to open up to Jesus as a best friend.

Where: Creating a personal friendship with Jesus is much like creating a friendship with anyone else. If you have an earthly best friend, think back to when you first met that person. I'm sure that you weren't thinking that they were going to be your best friend. Building that friendship took time and intentionality. There were disagreements and periods of silence, maybe even thoughts of ending the friendship. However, you were both able to navigate those rough times, and now your friendship is solid and thriving.

Building a solid personal friendship with Jesus is the same. It will take time and intentionality on your part to open up to Him and to listen to what he has to tell you. It is very difficult to be friends with someone who always talks about themselves and never quiets down to let someone else talk. It's also difficult to be close friends with someone who always thinks they are right and never wants to hear advice or take loving, honest criticism. In the same way, do not be that type of friend to Jesus. Remember, this is the only friend who actually died on the cross for you. So be sure to approach the friendship with honor and respect.

When: Once you have a well-established friendship with Jesus, it should last the remainder of your years here on earth. It should also be a great preface to being with Him in Heaven. Just like any other friendship, your friendship with Jesus must be maintained. There is no set time and place when it comes to getting personal with Him. This is what makes Him the ultimate best friend. He is available anytime; therefore, He doesn't need to check His schedule, check with His spouse, or wait until the kids go down for a nap. When you need to talk, He is always there for you. Feel free to get personal during your lunch break or while grocery shopping. Let go of the idea that you may ever inconvenience God or get on His nerves. I know that as earthly parents we have a tendency to feel this way toward our children, but God is the perfect Father who is always willing to listen to us.

Why: So many people look at God like He is some mystical character way up in the sky. They act as if He is too far away to care about us on a personal level, and that He is really only waiting for us to mess up. That can't be further from the truth. A personal friendship with the living God is very tangible and available to all who accept Him into their life and heart. We often give the number one spot in our hearts to things that do not belong there. Give your friendship with Jesus the number one spot in your life. Afterall, it is from Him that all things flow.

Let's Connect it to Scripture:

♥ Acts 17:28 – "For in Him we live and move and exist. As some of your own poets have said, 'We are His offspring.' "
♥ John 15:14-15 – "You are my friends if you do what I command. I no longer call you slaves, because a master doesn't confide in his slaves. Now, you are my friends, since I have told you everything the Father told me."
♥ James 4:8 – "Come close to God and God will come close to you. Wash your hands you sinners; purify your hearts, for your loyalty is divided between God and the world."

Let's Walk it Out:

Are you ready to get personal with Jesus? Now is the time to lay it all out. Take some time to pray now, and tell God you want a closer friendship with Him. Allow Him to show you anything that may be holding you back from experiencing closeness with Him. Write it down below, and then ask God to remove that hindrance.

_____

_____

_____

_____

_____

Sign _____

Date_____

Let's Write it Out:

1. What have today's scriptures revealed to you about who God is?

2. What old mindsets about friendship do you need to renounce so that you can be free to get close and personal with Jesus as your best friend?

Let's Pray it Out:

Wonderful Father, Counselor, and Friend, I praise and worship you for who you are. Lord, I confess that I have been fearful to get too close to you. Lord, I want that to change today. Father, I ask that you would remove any old mindsets or hindrances in my life that would keep me away from you. Thank you, Lord, that I am yours and that nothing can change that. Lord, I am ready to become best friends with you. Amen.

Day Twenty-Five

Know That You are Loved

Let's talk about love. It seems that our culture today has really made a mockery of love. It's become such a loose term. We love a certain celebrity, we love more than one person, we love this, and we love that. I'm convinced that the way in which the word love is thrown around today is extremely far and different from how God desired it to be used. The sad truth is that most people today do not even believe in love anymore. It's been so watered down, so twisted, and so flipped that people know it's not the real deal. Yet, instead of seeking out real love, people have allowed themselves to conform to culture's new definition of it. Conforming is easy, especially when you're going along with the majority. Still, if you watch the majority, you will see that they don't care about love anymore. The only thing they care about is themselves.

So, how do you live in a world that tells you to only care for yourself, regardless of what's going on around you? It can be difficult to find, but people are actually thirsty for real love again. They've seen the damage, and they've felt the pain of this artificial love. Now, they want to know what's real. The beauty of this is that, as believers, we have the opportunity to show them that real love still exists and can be found by anyone who wants to receive it. It starts with you. I know it's intimidating to think that you can create change all by yourself, but don't let the lie of the enemy get into your head. God wants to use you to display His glory and love to a hurting and dying world. You are not alone in this journey. He is with you, and He will bring others alongside you at the right time. Remember that you are a part of a large body, and you will need all of your other parts to operate in God's love. Soon, you'll be riding deep with a team of people that will help you display God's true love.

In order to display His love to others, you first have to know, understand, and believe that you are loved. This part may be a long and difficult journey for some women, especially if they've been under the trickery of the world's love. If that is you, take some time to heal first. God knows what happened to you. He feels your pain, and He knows it was not your fault and that it was only a by-product of this sinful world. Remember that there are women all over the world suffering right now from the very thing that God has rescued you from recently. He can take anything the enemy means for bad and turn it into a victory for you. Go to Him for healing so that you can reach out and grab the women that are still out there lost.

When you are in a place where you know that you are loved feverishly, then you are able to operate from a place of love. This is the way that you show a hurt and dying world the love of Jesus. Many times, people reserve love for only their family members or friends, but love is for everyone. Just as Jesus loves us all, we are also called to love. This means not just loving the people that you like, but also those that are difficult to like. It does not mean that you must be friends with everyone or accept the sin in their lives. It simply means that you should operate from a place of love when dealing with anyone. Allow love to motivate your actions towards people.

Let's Break it Down:

How: Operating out of love is not a suggestion. It is a requirement, a commandment by God that we, as believers, must follow. It's not always an easy thing to do, but we have to give it our best effort. Remember, when you are operating out of love there is no room for fear, anxiety, or anger. The homeless man on the street, the woman selling her body on the corner, or the couple who has fallen victim to drug abuse are all as equally important to God as you are. Yes, their sins are ugly, but so were yours before God rescued you. You still sin today; however, now you are aware of His grace, love, and forgiveness. God wants these people to know what you know. He wants to rescue them, too. So purpose in your heart to act and respond out of love towards everyone. Ask God to give you His heart for people. He will steer you towards loving others in a way that honors Him.

What: Do you know that you are loved? The biggest evidence of this is that Jesus died a very bad death on the cross for you. This was way before you were even born. He knew that you were coming and that you would be a sinful mess in need of a savior. Therefore, He willingly died so that you could live with Him forever. Real, true love is so powerful. You should be aware that there are different types of love. There are four I will cover briefly. *Storge* is an affection love shared between family members. *Philia* is a friendship love. *Eros* is a romantic love that is shared between married couples. *Agape* love is the love of God it is an unconditional, never-ending love. It is agape love that brought Jesus to the cross. (www.godandscience.org)

Where: It is a big misconception that love is a feeling generated from the heart. Most people think that if they do not feel love, then it's not love. Contrary to popular belief, true love has nothing to do with feelings or the heart. It is actually a commitment to act and operate out of love whether it is felt or not. Love may most definitely have feelings attached to it, but it will not be singularly guided by that feeling.

When: In life, it will be necessary at one point or another to be able to exercise all the forms of love. It is agape love that you should have towards God. This type of love says, "I will love you no matter what and no matter the cost, because you are worth it." Philia love will be the love that draws in close friends who will walk alongside you and share an emotional connection with you. Storge love will bind you together with your immediate family and your spiritual family. Eros love is reserved for your spouse and serves to fuel the fire of passion that connects you to each other. Love solidified in commitment will always prompt action sometimes in absence of feelings. This should be the foundation from which we operate with anyone. So, you may not have any type of romantic or friendship feelings towards the homeless man, but because God loves him, you love him. Subsequently, you act upon that love and the move of the Holy Spirit by giving him food or money or stopping to pray with him. It may not be comfortable, it may not be popular, and it may look weird to others. Nevertheless, love doesn't care, because it's operating out of the heart of a God who first loved you. (www.godandscience.org)

Why: Because God said so. Period.

Let's Connect it to Scripture:

♥ John 13:34 – "So now I am giving you a new commandment: Love each other. Just as I have loved you, you should love each other."
♥ Romans 13:8 – "Owe nothing to anyone - except for your obligation to love one another. If you love your neighbor, you will fulfill the requirements of God's law."
♥ 1 Peter 4:8 – "Most important of all, continue to show deep love for each other, for love covers a multitude of sins."

♥ Luke 10:27 – "The man answered, 'You must love the Lord your God with all your heart, all your soul, all your strength, and all your mind.' And love your neighbor as yourself."

♥ John 3:16 – "For this is how God loved the world: He gave His one and only Son, so that everyone who believes in Him will not perish but have eternal life."

Let's Walk it Out:

Sister, you are loved, and now it's time to walk in it. Take some time to pray and ask God to share with you how He wants you to operate in love towards others. Write His response below:

_____

_____

_____

_____

_____

_____

Sign _____

Date _____

Know That You are Loved

Let's Write it Out:

1. What have today's scriptures revealed to you about who God is?

2. In what ways have you witnessed the love of Christ in others, and how has it influenced you as a believer?

3. What does it mean to you to know that Jesus was willing to be killed on a cross to pay for all your sins and spend eternity with you in Heaven?

Let's Pray it Out:

Lord, you are mighty to save and awesome in power. Because of you, I am the head and not the tail. You go before me and provide a way. I confess that my attitude and behavior towards others has not always been loving. I have struggled with love and being loved, but I am ready to be healed and free. Lord, I invite you into the dark and hurting places within me, and I ask that you would take the pain and the anger and replace it with the soothing presence of your Holy Spirit. I want to be a vessel of your love to a hurt and dying world. Lord, may they see your love in me and through my actions. Amen.

Day Twenty-Six

Rock Your Crown

Sister, you look beautiful in your crown. Yes! I'm talking to you. You are royalty, after all. The image of a crown denotes such regality. It sits high upon the head; it glistens with precious stones and fine metals. It is something that every little girl dreams of wearing as a princess. There's something about wearing that crown, being dressed in a beautiful gown, and being looked upon with adoration that tugs at the heart of every young girl. It's a fantasy we've all spent hours dreaming upon and drooling over as we watched countless reruns of princess movies. However, it's time for you to wake up! There is no longer a need for you to dream and drool. The day you accepted Jesus into your life as your Lord and Savior, you were adopted into royalty. This is the most royal family that there will ever be, and you now are the princess you always dreamed of being.

Have you ever taken notice to how people treat someone who wears a crown? The crown alone denotes respect, value, and importance. Usually, before anything about a person is even revealed, the crown leads others to believe this is a person of privilege and authority. What is it about a crown that makes people behave with such reverence? Let's take a moment to consider the ancient meaning behind a crown. In history, a crown symbolized power, victory, and legitimacy. People who are raised in a royal lineage are usually taught to walk a certain way, talk a certain way, and behave a certain way. They must carry on a time-honored tradition of royal mannerisms. They have a duty to uphold the foundation laid from generations before them, and they must continue to lead in triumph for the generations that will follow them.

Well, it is time for you to rock your crown. It is time for you to know your worth and value as a princess in God's royal family. As a little girl growing up, I did not learn about my own worth and value. I spent a lot of time in my teenage years trying to discover my own beauty. Because I didn't know my own beauty, I was gauging beauty through everyone else's lens. Whatever other girls were doing, whatever they were wearing seemed to make them look so confident, and they got so much attention. I wanted that same confidence and attention, and I felt like I had to copy what they were doing in order to get it. I spent years going through my adult life trying to be someone that I thought people would like. It was the biggest mystery to me. I let everything people said or didn't say affect who I was or who I thought I was. Even after being saved for many years, I struggled with being what everyone else thought was a "good Christian," instead of just being who God made me to be. As a child of God, I was not rocking my crown. He had already spoken identity over me, but I wasn't listening because I was too busy trying to please the wrong person. People of royalty have no time to entertain the noise of their haters or follow the crowd. They have work to do. Because they come in many forms, it can be all too easy to allow distractions to deter us away from our royal path. However, when you know you are royalty and when you know you have an empire to build, you become unstoppable.

The book of Esther comes to mind when I think of royalty. She is another powerhouse woman of God who accepted her position and played it well. Although she was fearful at first, when it was time to make a hard decision she did not allow the fear to control her or keep her paralyzed from moving forward. She had access to wise council, and she quickly realized there was much more at stake than her own well being. Because of her preparation for royalty, she knew how to handle the situation. She maintained her position with grace and strength. She accepted the responsibility of her position, she fasted for spiritual insight, and she developed a plan. Then, she trusted God for the outcome. Even though there was a plot on her and her people's lives in the midst of everything she was doing, she did not let it stop her from doing what she had to do.

In the end, God turned every evil plot against Esther and her family onto the heads of their enemies. They were given a massive victory and placed in high honor. Because Esther chose to recognize the legitimacy of her crown (both physical and spiritual) and walk in it, she was elevated to another level, and her blessings spilled over to her family and people. Being royalty is a high-calling that stretches beyond where you can see. Imagine if Esther would've been too afraid to rock her crown. Her life story shows us that when we walk in the position God has for us, big blessings follow. God never gives you an unneeded position. He's not the God of bench-warmers. He put you on the royal team, and He wants you to play your heart out. Just like every position of a basketball team is necessary whether big or small, your position in God's royal family is needed no matter how small you think it is. Play your position, rock your crown like a boss, and watch God elevate what you thought was no big deal.

Let's Break it Down:

How: Rocking your crown is a self-expression that comes from the Holy Spirit. It's not conceit, it's not ego, and it is not pride. It's an inner confidence birthed through the reality of who you are in Christ. Rocking your crown will be specific to you. You won't be rocking your crown like the sister next to you, and that's ok. There's room for all of God's royal family. Because of this, there is no need to fight or push for your position. Your place is your place, and no one can take it away from you.

What: Your crown is beautiful. Take some time to revel in it. Embrace it. Ask yourself, "Am I walking in royalty?" How do you see yourself? The way that you see yourself is the way that others will also see you. Power, victory, and favor are legitimately yours. When you begin to behave like royalty, you will change the atmosphere wherever you go. People may not always like it, but that doesn't change who you are. Royalty remains royal regardless of opposition. Learn to exercise your crown with grace and strength. When this happens, whatever you say and whatever you do shows that you will maintain your position no matter what the doubters in life think.

Where: You are needed, and your gifts are needed. You could literally be traveling the world sharing a message that God has put on your heart, or you could be penning it to a book. Your crown could take you places you've only dreamed about and put you before people you never thought possible. However, you have to put it on first. You have to accept the responsibility of the crown. Yes, responsibility. Even with all the privileges that come with royalty, I've never heard anyone say that it was easy. There will be hard decisions to make and battles to fight. In fact, everything won't always be about you. Still, no matter how difficult it gets, never take off your crown. No one can wear it like you. Your crown is your birthright as a child of God.

When: Today! Put your crown on now. Don't waste any more time being a version of yourself that God didn't intend you to be. Your friends may not be able to recognize you anymore. Your family may ridicule you, but it doesn't really matter. When you are being elevated to a new level, and when you are being poised for your royal distinction, people are going to notice. They may be afraid of this new you. They may even be jealous. Love them anyway, but don't let them hold you back from what God needs you to do. God will guide you to your royal team where you will experience support and encouragement. It may not include the people you'd like it to include, but don't try to hold onto people that God already knows can't go where you're going.

Why: I know you're probably thinking of the little (or big) world changer(s) sitting under your own roof right now. You know they are watching everything, your every step. Everything you are doing now is establishing a foundation for them to build upon later. Be sure that you are leading them to a triumphant procession. Rock your crown so that you can help teach them how to rock theirs.

Let's Connect it to Scripture:

♥ Esther 4:14 "And who knows but that you have come to royal position for such time as this?"
♥ 2 Timothy 2:21 – "If you keep yourself pure, you will be a special utensil for honorable use. Your life will be clean, and you will be ready for the Master to use you for every good work."
♥ Isaiah 62:3 – "The Lord will hold you in His hand for all to see – a splendid crown in the hand of God."
♥ Hebrews 12:1 – "Therefore, since we are surrounded by such a huge crowd of witnesses to the life of faith, let us strip off every weight that slows us down, especially the sin that so easily trips us up. And let us run with endurance the race God has set before us."

Let's Walk it Out:

Are you ready to start rocking your crown? Since royalty is part of your inheritance as a child of God, how can you begin to walk in the position God has for as His daughter? Seek Him in prayer, and write His response below:

_____

_____

_____

_____

_____

_____

Sign _____

Date _____

Let's Write it Out:

1. What have today's scriptures revealed to you about who God is?

2. Mindset can play a heavy role in blocking the royal vision God has for you. What mindset about who you are, what you've done, or where you came from may be blocking you from seeing yourself as royalty in God's Kingdom?

3. Who you surround yourself with is important. Are there any people in your life that may not be able to go with you where God is trying to take you? Pray and ask God to give you fresh vision about the people in your circle.

Let's Pray it Out:

Lord, thank you for the many blessings you have given me and the many more blessing that you lovingly want to pour out. I ask that you would help me change my mindset. I want to live out life as the daughter of the King. I no longer desire to chase the wiles of men. I pray that you would remove anyone from my life that would keep me from the royal destiny you have for me. Lord, teach me how to rock my crown with grace and strength. Amen.

Day Twenty-Seven

Be a Blessing

Today's world has developed a culture that encourages everything and everyone to be self-absorbed. It is rare to find many people who will do anything for others unless it will benefit them in some kind of way. With all the many talents, gifts, and skills we've all been blessed with, most people are too self-centered to realize that these profound abilities were given as a way to bless others. In fact, our very lives were given to us to live out a life of servanthood to the people around us. It was never God's idea that we would scurry about seeking fame, accolades, and fortune just to please and satisfy our own selfish desires.

Jesus is Son of the King Almighty. He could have come to the Earth with a big bang wearing a crown and fine linens. Instead, Jesus stooped low. He was born in a barn around animals. His earthly mother and father were not of wealth. In those days, Jesus was considered to have a lowly appearance. He spent most of His life serving others. He was healing people, praying for people, and teaching people. He did not do it to enlarge His own ego or to be able to show how mighty He was. He did it all for His father - our Father. He did it all to give glory to God. Jesus did not once seek personal gain, and He very well could have for He is the Son of God, seated at the right hand of the Father. Instead, Jesus was kind. He saw injustice and pain, and He was emotionally and physically moved to help by love.

It is important that we look at Jesus' life on Earth and seek to develop His heart. He was always a leader, but He did not lead in the way that the world was accustomed to at the time. Therefore, many people did not want to recognize Him for who He was and still is. Jesus led by being a servant. He had a servant's heart. Often times, when we hear the word servant, we think of something really bad. Today, everyone is all about freedom and doing whatever feels good. As a result, a servant heart, as our world would define it, would be considered a poor and undesirable existence. However, this couldn't be farther from the truth.

Today, I want you to challenge the way you think when it comes to serving others. I actually like to call it being a blessing. It's an idea that I first personally learned and studied while in college. It's called being a Servant-Leader. (www.greenleaf.org) This is a powerful movement in leadership that operates from shared power and putting the needs of others first. This type of leadership is designed to help people develop and perform to their best abilities. Now, think back to a time when you were in need and someone helped meet that need for you. Maybe they gave you some money to pay a bill or some help carrying groceries. Maybe it was even someone who took time out of their day to sit and talk with when you needed a friend. Can you think back to how you felt before the need was met, and then how you felt afterwards? I'm sure that it brings two completely different emotions forth. I like to call it being blessed. Whenever someone does something to help me, whether it's needed or not, I feel completely blessed.

Now, *blessed* is another word that today's culture has redefined. What I am speaking of is the inner joy that comes from knowing God sees and cares for you. He cares for you so much, in fact, that He uses those around you who are obedient to Him as an extension of His heart. Being a blessing to others is all about you being obedient to God and allowing Him to use you as an extension of His heart to and for those around you. In Jesus' time, feet washing was a well-known part of cleansing. During those days, people only had sandals and had to walk everywhere. Consequently, their feet would get very dirty. Upon entering a home, one would remove their sandals and wash their feet. In richer homes, feet washing was done by a servant. It was not considered to be one of the most glamorous duties, but Jesus washed His disciple's feet. It was in response to love from God that outpoured from Jesus' own heart that He did this. It was the humble act of a servant who wanted to bless His people with a duty that would have been considered beneath Him. It was an action that would serve to inspire His people (the disciples and you and me) to do such things for others as an act of love.

Let's Break it Down:

How: Being a blessing to others does not require you to do anything extravagant. First and foremost, you must spend time with God and Hear His voice. As a result, everything you do will simply be in response to what He puts on your heart. Realize that you cannot be everything to everyone. It is a weakness of the flesh to think that we are able to be a savior to anyone. Renounce this lie and seek to only bless as God would have you to do so.

Be a Blessing

Please do not fall prey to blessing others under the façade of vanity and calling it Christ. To be an extension of God's heart, you must truly be in tune with God's heart. You must be surrendered to hearing His voice, and then obeying it.

What: There are some people that think being a good servant will get them into Heaven, make people like them, or that it will give them position to fix people's problems. This is not how being a blessing works. It is not your job, nor will it ever be, to seek to fix anyone. Remember to always stay within your boundaries, be careful not to cross over into territory that is not yours. It is only Christ who has the ability to heal and change people. Now, He often uses us in some way to do that, but it is never for our glory, and it is never us who truly makes it happen. It is only possible when we allow God to work through us.

Where: God loves to pour out His blessings on people, saved and unsaved. This is why you cannot be a judge guided by your own heart on who and when to bless. It is often the case that being a blessing to others will require sacrifice on your part. Too many times, people mistake being a blessing to others as some feel good, pay-it-forward kind of action. It can sometimes be that. However, in most cases, being a blessing to others requires placing your needs before someone else's in some way. This is why becoming an extension of God's heart can occur anywhere and may not look the way that you would always anticipate. Follow God's heart, and you will never go wrong - regardless of the sacrifice made on your end.

When: Being an extension of God's heart for others does not run on your own timing. God's timing is always perfect because He is perfect. This is regardless of how you feel about it or what you think you know. God does not change who He is, and He never will. So do not be held captive by timing. Do not allow the anxiety of when to bless someone make you worry. Truthfully, do not even allow the response of who you are trying to bless discourage you. There may be times when God leads you to bless someone that is totally unthankful or rude. Pay no attention to this. Realize that He knew their reaction beforehand, and that you do not bless for the praise of people. Always understand that there is something deeper going on that you may not see. Remember the trees and the forest, and just be obedient to plant whenever God says to do so. Then, trust Him with the overall outcome, for He is the one who brings forth the harvest.

Why: Jesus, King of Kings and Lord of Lords, had so much love in His heart that He would willingly stoop low and wash the feet of His disciples. This act of love and service was not done just to teach them how to bless others, but also to teach us. It is with this very heart attitude that you should desire to bless others. Seek to build up others, and allow your own selfish desires to be overtaken by the love of Jesus. As you honor Him, He will bless you.

Let's Connect it to Scripture:

♥ Isaiah 53:2 – "My servant grew up in the Lord's presence like a tender green shoot, like a root in a dry ground. There was nothing beautiful or majestic about his appearance, nothing to attract us to Him."
♥ Matthew 6:4 – "Give gifts in private, and your Father who sees everything, will reward you."
♥ 1 Peter 5:6 – "So humble yourselves under the mighty power of God, and at the right time He will lift you up in honor."
♥ John 13:12-15, 17 – "After washing their feet, He put on His robe again and sat down and asked, 'Do you understand what I was doing? You call me 'Teacher' and 'Lord,' and you are right, because that's what I am. And since I, your Lord and teacher, have washed your feet, you ought to wash each other's feet. I have given you an example to follow. Do as I have done to you. Now that you know these things, God will bless you for doing them.'"

Be a Blessing

Let's Walk it Out:

It's time to be a blessing, so let's get practical. Let's take a minute now to pause and pray. Ask God to show you someone that you can bless today. It may be a word of encouragement. It may be a stranger in the supermarket. Whatever you get, don't dismiss it. Write it down, and then obey.

_____

_____

_____

_____

_____

_____

Sign _____

Date _____

Let's Write it Out:

1. What have today's scriptures revealed to you about who God is?

2. How can you take what you've read in this chapter and pass it on to your children so that they learn to be an extension of God's heart? Pray about how God would like you to do this.

Let's Pray it Out:

Heavenly Father, your ways are always perfect. You are kind and slow to anger. Lord, I know that there are many hurt people who need to know that you love them dearly. I want to be an extension of your heart to those people. Thank you Lord, that you chose me and that you want to use me. Help me to teach and show my children how to be a blessing in word and action. Amen.

Day Twenty-Eight

Never Forget Your Roots

When we think of the word *past* it's natural that we would probably think of something that is gone by or doesn't exist anymore. For most of us, there's a part of our past that we'd like to completely forget, as if it never even happened. I know that the pain of certain experiences can be paralyzing and debilitating. Some incidents take years and years to recover from, and that's ok. I have an encouraging word to share with you: You're still here, and that means that your story is not over! God has more for you. It's always important to our spiritual walk to get healing from any unpleasant experiences, but also never forget that you serve a Mighty God. He makes all things new, which means He can give your pain purpose.

I know it's a concept that can be hard to grasp at first. However, God promises that it can all work out for your good if you just love and trust Him. When it comes to your past, you must be healed from it but not afraid of it. Healed says, "Yes, this happened to me, and it was a terrible thing - but God." Yet, fear says, "Yes, this happened to me, and it was a terrible thing. I don't want to think about it ever again." The contrast is that a healed voice admits what happened and gives the pain and all the other bad feelings to God so He can heal the wounds and bring forth something beautiful. On the other hand, a fearful voice knows something bad happened, but it doesn't want to deal with it. Therefore, it keeps it quiet and stuffed down, hoping it never comes up again so they don't have to feel the pain.

A fearful voice has worked hard to block out the pain, but that same pain blocking wall is also keeping out the soothing of the Holy Spirit. The fearful person never gives God a chance to heal them and make them new. At some point in the process of traumatic experiences, I believe we all have a heavy wall up against everything. I know I did. The problem is that when we get so used to operating that way, there comes a point when we no longer realize that there's a wall even there. It becomes normal to create emotional distance between ourselves and others. We feel the sting of loneliness, and we drown in the rush of our own thoughts. We become an island inhabited only by us, talking to sports balls with faces drawn on them. We think we look normal to the outside world, but everyone can tell that something's not right.

It takes a seed of humility to allow God to heal you, but it is worth it. That is why the work of healing must be done to completion. It is important for you to heal from the hurts of your past, but never forget where your roots are. So many times people overcome poverty, pain, and injustice, and then they walk away from that life into a new life and never look back. I do not mean for them to look back in regret or longing for the past, but to look back and see who is still there. When God brings you out of something, it is wise to have a humble heart and realize that it was God who did it and not you. This humble posture keeps your heart in right position for God to continue to use you. Stay humble and never forget your roots. Never forget the pain and hurt you went through. Even though you have made it to the other side, there are still plenty of people who have not. They are all waiting for someone like you - someone that God has rescued, healed and transformed and who knows exactly what kind of life they are trying to escape. That someone is you. If you refuse to heal and if you refuse to embrace humility, how can God use you to help someone else?

Let's Break it Down:

How: I understand it's tough to deliberately think about the bad things that have happened to you, but in order to find God in the mess, it is necessary. When you have allowed God to heal you of the pain, it is more bearable to look back on situations without feeling like you are experiencing them all over again. For me, never forgetting my roots means never forgetting how I felt when I became a single mom at twenty-one. I no longer feel that way, but because I can access that time in my life and see what God has done, I can share with women who feel the way that I used to feel. I can encourage them to know Jesus and be awakened to the revelation that God still loves them and their lives are not over. This is how you find purpose in your pain. It is my desire to share my personal struggles with others in hopes that it will deter them from a dangerous road, a road I once traveled.

What: Humility is the key to finding purpose in the pain. You have to be able to look beyond yourself and your own hurts and pains, and realize that Jesus is the only one who can restore you. The walk of humility has not been an easy one for me. For years, I sought to find my place in the world as a single mom. I felt alone, misunderstood, and devalued. Therefore, I slept around and became a heavy drinker in an attempt to find my place somewhere and be somebody. Pride kept me from forgiving myself and allowing God to heal me. Pride told me I could figure it out on my own. I let pride lie to me for years before I realized that God was the only real answer.

Where: Purpose is not always found in pain, but pain is a way that God can reveal purpose. Learn to be comfortable with who you are. I realize now that even though I never wanted to or planned to be a single mom, God has richly used that experience to develop me into the woman I am today. I am confident that had I not had my daughter, I would be in a completely different life. It would not necessarily be a good one. Know that God is always leading you on a triumphant journey. He didn't die just for you; He died for everyone else in this world, also. So, release pride, and allow God to use you and everything that you went through to expose His goodness to others.

When: God's timing is perfect. You will know when He is calling you out. In the meantime, be obedient to His preparation in your life. Remember to stay on the course and trust the process, even though you are not sure what He's doing. A mutual friend once linked me up with a lady who was a prayer warrior. We communicated through email periodically, and it was such a blessing to be in connection with her. We were spiritually contending for each other even though we were complete strangers. I was having a hard time one day and sent her fiery email to share what was going on in my life. I'll never forget her email back. It simply stated that "I needed to remember that God was always working even though I don't see it at times." Now I'm passing this golden nugget on to you. For me, it was another meeting with humility. Even when things are not going your way, you should still leave it in the hands of our all-capable God. It is not your job to decide when you are healed and ready to go back for others. When God's says you're ready, then you're ready -even if you don't feel like it. Until then, learn to walk in humility and know that you didn't get to where you are on your own. You won't get to where you need to be on your own either.

Why: My daughter likes to tell me that there is a *why* for every *why*. It's a game she plays with me sometimes. I'm not going to lie to you, this game can get kind of crazy at times. What I realized from it is that most people want to understand things. It's why science is so big these days. People want to make sense of what they don't understand. It seems that when people understand something or someone, they can accept it. However, when there is no understanding, major rejection occurs. Take a look at your old self - the girl trapped, lost, alone, and afraid. Where was she, what was she doing, what happened that brought about her rescue? It may not all make sense to you, and for some parts, you may never have full understanding. Still, accept that at one point you were that girl, and embrace who you now are. Then, know that there are still girls walking around trapped, lost, hurt, alone, and afraid. You know where to find them, because you know their roots.

Let's Connect it to Scripture:

♥ Proverbs 15:33 – "Fear of the Lord teaches wisdom; humility precedes honor."
♥ Philippians 2:3 – "Don't be selfish, don't try to impress others. Be humble, thinking of others as better than yourselves."
♥ Proverbs 11:2 – "Pride leads to disgrace but with humility comes wisdom."
♥ James 4:10 – "Humble yourselves before the Lord, and He will lift you up in honor."
♥ Romans 12:6 – "Live in harmony with each other. Don't be too proud to enjoy the company of ordinary people. And don't think you know it all."

Let's Walk it Out:

It's time for a change. Do you believe that God has the ability to birth purpose from your pain? Take some time now to pray and ask God to reveal His purpose in the pain you have experienced. Write down His response.

_____

_____

_____

_____

_____

_____

Sign _____

Date _____

Let's Write it Out:

1. What have today's scriptures revealed to you about who God is?

2. What has been something in your past that you have refused to allow God to properly heal and why?

3. What action do you need to take today so that you can be whole in Christ and available to answer His call? Think on this, and then pray for God's answer. It may be forgiving someone from your past, forgiving yourself for something you have done, or admitting that you are hurt and need Jesus to heal you.

Let's Pray it Out:
Lord, you are so loving, kind, and generous. I open my heart to you now and ask that you come in and heal the pain. I've carried it around so long, and I no longer want to hold on to it. Lord, I give you the pain, the anger, and the shame, and I receive your love, forgiveness, and grace. Forgive me for the pride I've held onto in my life. Heal me, Lord, and use me to go back to my roots and pull out those still trapped. Amen.

Day Twenty-Nine

Bloom Where You Are Planted

If you've ever been to a botanical garden, you know that it's a beautiful sight to see. There's all kinds of delicious pleasures for the eyes to behold. The trick is that you have to be able to slow down long enough to enjoy it. At first look, a lot of it may seem boring - especially if you're like me and you like to touch everything. Then, once you start really looking around and learning what's there, you start to realize how useful and interesting everything is. However, if you rush through it, you're bound to miss its true beauty.

I lived a few years of my life like this. I was on a timeline! My girl-friends and I had already discussed our plans for our lives. I was going to be married at twenty-five, have six kids, and live in a big house with two cars and dog. Oh, I forgot to mention that I was going to be the best stay-at-home mom. I planned to be cooking dinner nightly, entertaining friends, and running a highly successful business. Flash forward to reality, and that timeline is looking a lot different from what I planned.

Consequently, for years, I lived with a spirit of disappointment because nothing turned out the way that I wanted it to turn out. I had concluded that without the satisfaction of that timeline, there was nothing to enjoy about my life. My life was boring, and I had decided to just rush through the so-called uninteresting parts so that I could hurry up and get to the good stuff. Turns out, the "uninteresting" parts lasted a lot longer than I anticipated. And, I was forced to accept the fact that my timeline had vanished into thin air. However, this was a lie straight from the enemy, and it kept me from truly enjoying the beautiful life God had already given me.

In life, we all have that desire to find our purpose and live out our God-given destiny, but we first have to journey there, and then arrive. Even then, your purpose doesn't just stop there because your life is not a one-stop shop. You will never simply wake up and be at your destination. The good news is that as God's precious daughter, you are always right where He wants you, even if it doesn't seem like it. Moreover, I'm sure you're wondering, *"How do I enjoy the life I have now, even if it's not the timeline I had hoped for?"* The answer is as simple as is it profound: Be the woman in the botanical garden. No matter where on the "timeline" you find yourself, there is beauty to be seen. Bloom where you are planted so that when you move on, you will leave behind the beautiful scent of the Holy Spirit.

Let's Break It Down:

How: Blooming where you are planted requires a mindset shift. Just like a flower, it's a lot easier to bloom when it has fresh water and sunlight. The same thing goes for you. To promote blooming, start by reading your Word and spending time with God. Naturally, focusing on Him will not only cause you to bloom, but it will also change the way you see things. During the last few years of my current job, the Lord had really been teaching me about this. I went from coming into work every day dreading it and wishing I wasn't there, to going into work every day looking for physical and spiritual needs and asking God how I could be used. I still would rather not be there, but the difference is now I understand that He has me there for a reason because it's His timeline and not mine. Since I know it's not by mistake that I'm there, it makes me all the more eager to be used by Him right where I am. This is the essence of learning to bloom where you are planted.

What: Blooming is less about you and more about God. You are His daughter after all, and He does have a plan for you on His timeline. So, be careful not to take things into your own hands in an effort to speed Him up. Just like the walk around the botanical garden, there is a beauty to be found right where you are. Your timeline or not, you are useful and you are interesting. Most importantly, God is eager to work in you and through you. As long as you are willing, you can be assured that He will see to it that you bloom regardless of where He plants you.

Where: You're planted where you are for a reason. God doesn't do anything wasteful. He'll move you and expand your territory when He's ready and when He knows you're ready. The important thing is to stop and see where He has you now and why. Looking at the life of Jesus, we can see that He was always about His Father's business wherever He went. He was always blooming right where God had Him. Even in the rough times, He still chose

God's timeline over His own. When it was all said and done, God expanded His territory big time.

When: It took me some time to understand that it was a necessary part of my walk and growth as a believer to bloom where I was planted. Though, it may not take you as long to catch the hint. Hopefully, your desire is to work on blooming now rather than later. Think about who is in your life right now that God may be trying to use you to minister to or to encourage. Blooming isn't just about you, it's also about those around you. It could possibly be for you to bless the co-worker that you can't stand to be in the same room with for more than a few seconds. It could even be the neighbor who constantly plays loud music late into the night. As you consider the idea of blooming where you are planted, consider what Jesus may have called the "least of these" and how your blooming could impact their lives.

Why: As Christians, it is God's desire that we are always maturing. Blooming where you are planted is a big part of that. Imagine for a moment if Jesus had decided to rush through the moments of His life, failing to see what God was doing. Thank you, Jesus, that He didn't! Now, it's your turn. As He said in part of Luke 22:42, "Yet I want your will to be done, not mine."

Let's Connect it to Scripture:

♥ Luke 22:42 - "Father, if you are willing, please take this cup of suffering away from me. Yet I want your will to be done, not mine."
♥ Isaiah 50:7 - "Because the Sovereign Lord helps me, I will not be disgraced. Therefore, I have set my face like a stone, determined to do His will. And I know that I will not be put to shame.
♥ 2 Thessalonians 1:11 - "So we keep on praying for you, asking our God to enable you to live a life worthy of His call. May He give you the power to accomplish all the good things your faith prompts you to do."
♥ Psalm 51:10 - "Create in me a clean heart, O God. Renew a loyal spirit within me."
♥ Matthew 5:16 - "In the same way, let your good deeds shine out for all to see, so that everyone will praise your heavenly Father."

Let's Walk it Out:

Are you ready to see the botanical garden in your life? Pray and ask God to open your eyes so that you can see the beauty in your life. Ask Him to reveal how you can begin to bloom right where He planted you. Wait and listen, and then write His response below:

_____

_____

_____

_____

_____

_____

Sign _____

Date _____

Let's Write it Out:

1. What have today's scriptures revealed to you about who God is?

2. Are there any unresolved emotions that you have allowed to stunt your ability to bloom where you are planted? If so, take a moment to release those emotions to God. Allow Him to comfort you and fill you with His love.

Let's Pray It Out:

Heavenly Father, I am amazed by your love and care for me. How wonderful you are to me! Forgive me, Lord, for attempting to go against your plan for my life. Lord, all of your ways are perfect, and I surrender my life to your perfect plan for me. Let me see the beauty of the life you have given me. It is my desire to honor you and bloom where I am planted. Thank you for being a good Father to me. Amen

Day Thirty

Share Your Story

In closing this devotional, I want to encourage you to not be afraid to share your story. Your story is unique to you, and no one can ever discredit it. Believe it or not, your story even has power. I have to admit that I didn't even think I had a story to tell. For the longest time, I admired people who had something to share with me, and I wondered when I would have a story of my own. It wasn't until I allowed God to bring me up and out of the mess I was in that I was able to see that I had a story all along. Then, of course, I became afraid to share it. I wasn't sure of exactly what to say or to whom I should say it. I was afraid I would stumble over my words, while randomly spitting all over the person I was talking to at that moment.

As I began to connect with other women, I learned that sharing was just like having a conversation. I learned that I didn't have to share my whole entire life story with everyone I came in contact with on my journey. As the saying goes, "sharing is caring." Sharing my story was about seeing where someone else was and caring because I used to be there, too. It wasn't about fixing their problem or hard-selling them on Jesus. It was simply showing that I cared enough about them to open up and connect my story with their struggle.

People are longing to be loved and understood. When you share with someone struggling that you have been there too, and they can see how God changed you, it's a powerful thing. That alone is a seed planted in their heart. It may be that you never get to personally see that seed burst forth with fruit, but trust God that you did your part, and He'll take care of the rest. Share your story, and release the self-righteous attitude so that you can display humility and love as you allow Christ to work through you to reach a hurting person. At the end of the day, always make it all about Jesus, and you will never go wrong.

As part of my desire to be vulnerable and authentic with you, I would like to share a part of my story. It is nothing that I am proud of, but I know that many of you reading this are walking in the same shoes that I once knew well. Find encouragement to know that you don't have to stay there. We all have choices, and I pray that in reading my story, you will find the courage to choose to walk towards Jesus.

At the age of twenty-one, I became pregnant by a man who was married to another woman. I felt like all the dreams I had for myself were crushed in an instant. All at once, the years of pain, mistreatment, alcohol abuse, and sexual promiscuity had culminated into the very moment when I looked at myself and realized that I would be a single mom. I grew up in the church, I had heard the sermons, I had learned right from wrong, and yet I still ended up on the wrong path. I carried the shame of my sin around like a backpack full of rocks. My life was over. It was my fault entirely, and the dream I had of getting married and having a family full of kids had been destroyed by my disobedience and rebellion against God.

I was holding in so much pain from my youth and from adulthood. I didn't like myself, and so I didn't expect anyone else to like me either. I had no idea how to get away from the darkness and loneliness that I felt deep inside my heart. Although I felt far from God, I can now look back and see that He was still taking care of me. I was very far from home when I became a single mom, and there was no family around me. God brought two women into my life both older and wiser than I was. He gave me one that I could trust with my daughter. She helped me raise her and taught me stuff the parenting books didn't cover. The other lady became like a stand-in mom. She filled the gap where my mom could not physically be. She invited me to holiday dinners and spent time talking to me.

Still, I had not really dealt with the issues inside me. Instead, I found ways to make myself feel better. I tried to become a person that I thought others would like. I was desperate to be loved and fell trap to the advances of even more married men. I didn't know my worth. I didn't know how much Jesus loved me. I didn't know that He had a much better life for me, and that He wasn't angry at me. I eventually got back into church, but every time I did, a new guy would come along, and I would be lured away and back into my old ways of living time and time again. The pull with these men was so strong that I couldn't shake it. The only way it ever ended was bad, and then I was left bewildered with my heart torn to pieces, feeling angry and worthless.

This went on for years. It was a sick cycle of abuse I did to myself. At the end of another cycle, I again got back into church. This time, I was really enjoying it and wanting to change my life. I started getting discipled, and I was so excited. Then, a married man at work began to flirt with me.

I tried to get away from it, but again, I was pulled to him with his sad stories. I actually believed that he had married the wrong woman and was really my husband! I shared everything with the girl who discipled me, and she was supportive but firm in telling me that I was wrong and needed to stay away no matter what he said. However, I did not listen. I went full blown into a relationship with him.

My discipler warned me that if I didn't stop, she would be forced to bring it to the attention of someone for outside help, namely my pastors or my mom. I knew that being hard-headed to the many warnings that came before this had brought me to this rock-bottom place. However, I was still appalled that she would do this to me. I decided that if anyone was going to air my dirty laundry, it would be me. I'll never forget the Sunday that I sat with the pastors and told them what I had been doing. It was humiliating, but it broke the curse off me. From that day forward, I never had married men chasing me again, and I no longer was interested in them.

My journey began that day. It's been a slow process, but Jesus has been gentle with me every step of the way. With His help, I was able to break free from codependency and slowly come out of my shell. I started to see myself the way that He did. I started to believe that my life wasn't over, and that there were things that He still wanted me to do. I started to fall in love with Jesus. The deeper I got with Him, the more it changed me. I spent years searching for love in all the wrong places, and all along the love I needed - the love that would soothe my soul, heal my hurts, and make me beautiful - was in Jesus.

Today, I am not at all the girl I once was. I love who I am. I'm making friends with other Godly women, and God has been opening up so many doors in my life as He shows me the plans that He has for me. It's been a continual act of complete surrender to Him, but I'm growing, and His friendship is like no other. I still struggle with things, and I'm not perfect, but it's through my relationship with Him that I live out my life. I know and believe that God has amazing things in store for me. I know that my future with Him will be great.

It is because of His relentless pursuit of me that I can tell you what a horrible mess I was. It is because of His undying love for me that I pour out my heart before you, so that you can know that everything He did for me, He can do for you and more. Throughout all the different seasons in my life there have been Scriptures that have helped me and strengthened my relationship with the Lord. Today, I want to share these very special verses with you. I encourage you to discover verses that you can speak over your life, and I pray that you fall deeper in love with Jesus as you blossom into the woman you were always meant to be.

It is time for you to **Blossom**!

My Life Verses

Isaiah 40:31 - But those who trust in the Lord will find new strength. They will soar high on wings like eagles. They will run and not grow weary. They will walk and not faint.

Philippians 4:6-7 - Don't worry about anything instead, pray about everything. Tell God what you need, and thank Him for all He has done. Then you will experience God's peace, which exceeds anything we can understand. His peace will guard your hearts and minds as you line in Christ Jesus.

Deuteronomy 8:6-10 - So obey the commands of the Lord your God by walking in His ways and fearing Him. For the Lord your God is bringing you into a good landof flowing streams and pools of water, with fountains and springs that gush out in the valleys and hills. It is a land of wheat and barely; of grapevines, fig trees, and pomegranates of olive oil and honey. It is a land where food is plentiful and nothing is lacking. It is a land where iron is as common as stone, and copper is abundant in the hills. When you have eaten your fill, be sure to praise the Lord your God for the good land He has given you.

Romans 8:28 - And we know that God causes everything to work together for the good of those who love God and are called according to His purpose for them.

Psalm 63:1-8 - O God, you are my God: I earnestly search for you. My soul thirsts for you; my whole body longs for you in this parched and weary land where there is no water. I have seen you in your sanctuary and gazed upon your power and glory. Your unfailing love is better than life itself; how I praise you! I will praise you as long as I live, lifting up my hands to you in prayer. You satisfy me more than the richest feast. I will praise you with songs of joy. I lie awake thinking of you, meditating on you through the night. Because you are my helper, I will sing for joy in the shadow of your wings. I cling to you; your strong right hand holds me securely.

About the Author

Elaina Michelle is a writer, Dental Hygienist, Certified Health Coach and mom. She holds a bachelors degree in Human Development and has a heart to see single moms break free from their past to be mighty women of God. She hopes that through her writing she can encourage others and share the love of God. Elaina was born and raised in California. She loves spending time with her daughter, and is passionate about healthy eating and healthy living. You can reach her at michelleelaina@hotmail.com or visit www.royalnourishment.com.